TRAFFICKED IN PLAIN SIGHT

A Hybrid's Own War

Lisa Bramer

Copyright © 2024 Lisa Bramer
All rights reserved
First Edition

PAGE PUBLISHING
Conneaut Lake, PA

First originally published by Page Publishing 2024

ISBN 979-8-89157-523-3 (pbk)
ISBN 979-8-89157-546-2 (digital)

Printed in the United States of America

PROLOGUE

People come to the US for freedom and to live the American dream. While that may be true for some, not everyone gets to do so. I was born here, and I've always wished I could have been born in a different country. Today, people celebrate Juneteenth, the day it became a law that no one shall own slaves. According to my family, William Floyd did not want to give up his slaves. Is there anyone who can account for every slave William Floyd freed? I grew up being brought to parks and beaches in nearby towns to see where my body would be disposed of if I did not obey my family's German rules. They claim that is where slaves have gotten thrown to rot since slavery became illegal. So when celebrating this new holiday, that is what you are celebrating; the day historical cowards learned that they must keep their slaves hidden in plain sight to keep things as they were when people were allowed to enslave the innocent.

Then decades later, it became known that Adolf Hitler and his army of cowards were enslaving and murdering people. Some think one had nothing to do with the other; I think it was a new plan in the making, one to reclaim, so to speak, what is rightfully theirs. My ancestors, along with many other families, migrated to the US from England. Since then, the world has become more and more like hell on Earth. All the diseases that spread and kill innocent lives, all the "accidental" overdoses, car crashes leading to fatalities, the seeming suicides. While some are true to be, not all are. My family has made many claims about celebrities whose disappearances or suicides were murder and that the killers were allowed to kill. People die of cancer that spreads by some concoctions laced into their cigarettes without their knowledge. My mother was one of them since she left my abusive father, trying to save her children as it was unknown to her that when someone owns you, there is only one way out, death. My daughter's father did not commit suicide willingly. His father told him he should swallow pills. When he had not died, his father suggested drinking bleach. That also did not work, so he told him his last and final idea as another relative left the weapon to do so accessibly to him.

Too many lives have we lost to deadly viruses that spread worldwide, such as COVID-19. Back in 2015, my father worked for a pharmaceutical company. He gave me a pencil case with items inside, such as a pencil, eraser, and more that had the word Remdesivir on them. My father told me that, in time, it could save my life; all I must do is change my ways and follow in his path. Five years later, people started getting terminally ill and dying from the coronavirus. Had a certain law enforcement agent, the man who proudly walks in the shoes of the deceased Adolf Hitler, not paraded around about everything between having the virus and having the cure for it? I may not have figured it out as fast as I did. Once I saw that word, Remdesivir, I had a clear flashback of the day my father brought me that pencil case. I immediately picked up the phone and called the tip line. A few years later, and this agent is still walking free.

So when celebrating Juneteenth, ask yourself why you are celebrating and think about all the innocent lives lost while criminals get away with murder and mayhem. Why is a Nazi allowed to be in law enforcement? Why are outlaw biker gangs allowed to exist? It's not as if they try to hide it; they are proud of what they are. They share it with the whole world and then let everyone know "there is nothing" we can do to stop them. So you should not celebrate a day when slaves got set free because we never were. They do not call us slaves anymore; these days, we are called sluts. Criminals made up that word and what that "word" means so everyone would think she wanted it. And when we turn to drugs or alcohol to numb the pain of abuse, we are called addicts and considered losers and lowlifes or told we wouldn't go to heaven.

As I do not wish my life on even the evilest of them all, try imagining what it would be like to be burned as a baby, having the life beat out of you daily, and told you are stupid by many, being molested and raped repeatedly. Imagine being convicted of a sex crime as the predator is known as the victim. Then you are no longer allowed near your child. Then you are saved from being trafficked, fall in love, and get pregnant but told you must ask permission from a judge to keep your unborn child. And as relieved and thankful as you are when they permit you, you know that while you are allowed to have your second born, your firstborn has to stay away and can only speak to you once a week until your six-year probation has expired.

It began in May 2017; it ended in May 2023. Even though probation will end, you will still have to register as a sex offender until you turn sixty-two. And all this plus more happened to you because you chose to be a good person with a loving heart.

CHAPTER 1

A Chosen One Is Born

Life began for me at the end of 1983, given to my mother, Rosewitha Brewski, and my father, Adolfi Wolfgang Averbach. During my infant years, we lived in a two-story house on Stockton Rd. in Mystic Bay, New York. While I do not recall living there, things were happening that I can never forget. I had a big sister, Ada, born in the middle of 1981. She had the most mesmerizing blue eyes and blonde hair. I just loved her so much. I couldn't wait to be able to walk and talk just like her. I was eager to be able to play with her and her toys. I could not understand why, but our father and his family kept telling me that she was a natural-born slave and I must treat her like a slave. They repeatedly told me how God saw me even though I was not a boy as I was supposed to be since I was born with brown hair and eyes. God chose me to join in and not be a slave like most women are. But in turn, I must obey my father and our fathers before us.

My great-aunt, Bertha, was their example for me to learn. She owned a home on some land that William Floyd once owned, which I dreaded going to, seeing that my mother and sister were not pleased to go there either. It always felt like my father was driving his family to hell; a visitor will see a beautiful community, like a fairy tale. The lawns were always freshly cut and well-kept, and the roads were always clean. For those who have the slightest clue about what is beyond all the beauty, it would seem like a warm, loving place with wholesome families. However, when you remove the blinders you didn't even know were over your eyes, you will see all the abuse and hatred under the blanket of lies and deception. You will feel all the fake love around you; you will see all the sad faces of the people you thought were just landscapers or nannies for children or something in that sense. The children you see are hurt inside and out from the beatings they receive for disobeying their family's rules, longing for a warm, loving family that will raise them and not train them like some mini-war soldier.

In this beautiful community, there were men, women, and children who were beaten and or raped where your eyes couldn't see. Having known this, the whole ride to dear Great-Aunt Bertha's, even for a visit, was horrifying as I was this tiny, helpless baby, crying silently, asking God to save me from evil. And when we would pull up to my aunt's house, my body would feel numb and weak. Hearing my aunt offer my mother coffee was scary because I knew what was coming. My aunt lived with her husband, Hans, and his sister, Maple. They were nothing like my aunt. She enslaved them and used them as a distraction when she felt one needed disciplinary action.

Once my mother was deep into conversation enough that she wouldn't notice our disappearance, my sister and I would have to go into the room with a very depressing, dim light. My father would sit in the discipline chair after my aunt would say, "Adolfi, you know what you must do." I would have to sit on his lap as he would whip away with a belt. My sister would have to stand in front of the chair for her discipline. We didn't always go into the room together. When I didn't have my big sister, I had to watch sex on television to learn what I must do for my husband in the future. I was molded like clay to sit with one leg crossing the other, back arched so my butt protrudes outward. As painful as that was, I was not allowed to cry or face getting "something to cry for." My aunt always said, "Beauty is pain, so deal with it unless you want to be ugly like your slut mother and sister."

Since I had no choice but to keep going to a home of Satan, I thought of things to think about during my stay that would resemble some sense of love and kindness. My aunt had a beautiful backyard where my sister loved running around as her pin-straight blonde hair followed behind her. I loved when she'd dress in white because she looked like an angel, the most beautiful angel I ever saw. I thought about how much I love my uncle Hans and aunt Maple and how they love and respect my mother and sister just as much as me. I admired how they were like my mother and sister; even though they lived in misery, they stayed strong and brave. These kind people always had smiling faces whenever they could as if their lives were perfect.

My great-aunt took advantage of their caring hearts and took for granted that without them, she wouldn't have been able to live with having a disability due to developing arthritis in both hands. Who would cook for her and help her get dressed when she had difficulty doing so?

At some point, my family and I moved into a new apartment in a white house that I thought to be a castle as my family considered me a princess. Even the evil people called me that too. Our landlords lived on the lower level while we lived on the top. Their names were Joseph and Lynette, and they had a daughter, Rebecca. I wanted them to be my family and to help me save my daddy from following the devil.

When the weather warmed up in 1985, my father brought his family to an Indian reservation in New York. There we would visit a man my father treated like a dear friend. His name was Barry; he owned a hot dog truck. Like our landlord, he was very kind and welcoming. It hurt me when my father would say bad things about these wonderful people when they weren't around to hear it. I was tired of hearing about world wars from before I was born and how I must prepare for WW3 in the future. I decided that as soon as I could talk, I would tell these kind human beings that God brought into my life, and we would prepare for our army to fight against the Germans and all the other racist people who want to be evil. Then when the time came, I would send them back to their own country. Only then will the ones I love be able to live free and truly happy.

Once I began to be able to say some words, like mommy, daddy, and sissy, I decided I would make my aunt and uncle happy and proud of me. We were visiting Great-Aunt Bertha, and I walked right up to Uncle Hans and Aunt Maple and said their respective names as best as I could, "Un An, An Ma." They were so happy and hugged me, and then I heard, "Rosewitha, would you like a cup of coffee?"

My stomach began to hurt, and not long after, I was getting my discipline. This time though, Grandpa Wilheim was visiting too, and he asked his son to give him a few minutes with me. After my father left the room, Grandpa began touching me most uncomfortably. He "ever so" gently rubbed my arms, barely touched my skin, leaving me with this horrifying chill, and moved to my legs. As Grandpa continued to caress me, he claimed that if I wanted to consider those slaves my aunt and uncle, I would have to be a dirty slave just like them. Then Grandpa made me play "hobby horse" but not Daddy's version of the hobby horse game. No, that was fun; I had to sit on my grandfather's lap with my back arched so my vagina would rub against his leg as he bounced me forcefully up and down. Finally, he had finished his form of discipline, and we were allowed to join everyone in the area they were in.

Looking undeniably sad, my mother asked me what was wrong. My great-aunt told her that she let me play with her dolls and that I was deliberately disrespecting them. My mother didn't question her. At home, whenever I played with my toys, I would have a favorite in one hand and one that I least liked in the other as I would make them fight, and then I'd fling the least favorite across the room. When my sister saw this, it would make her laugh, and that made me happy because she didn't know that I was creating an army to save her and everyone we love from the evil Germans. I was training myself to fight against them while trying my hardest to make them believe I was on their side. My mother automatically assumed that was what I just did with my aunt's expensive collection of porcelain dolls, which, had I broken one, she couldn't afford to replace.

Later, when serving dessert in the dining room, as Aunt Maple went to place a bowl of my favorite ice cream, mint chocolate chip, in front of me, Aunt Bertha intervened and grabbed it from her. I had to sit at the table and watch everyone enjoy their dessert, hoping my daddy would give in and let me have some of his. Deep down, I knew that was only something he'd do at our home, so I kept telling myself we would be going home soon, and before I knew it, we were saying our goodbyes.

CHAPTER 2

Growing Up Adolfi

Adolfi was born mid-1960. He was brought up by his father, Wilheim Averbach, and his grandfather, also named Wilheim; to know that, since he was born with blond hair, he was a natural-born slave. His mother, Daisy, was enslaved by these men and was purposely misdiagnosed with schizophrenia and bipolar disorder, being put on medications she didn't need to take. Adolfi had two older siblings, Heinrich and Jakob. A couple of years after Adolfi was born, he and his brothers got a new baby sister, Anna. As they grew, Adolfi despised his oldest brother, Heinrich, but he loved his brother, Jakob, and their sister, Anna, unconditionally just as he had their mother. Adolfi couldn't understand why he was constantly getting abused by his father and grandfather or had to watch or listen to his mother and siblings endure abuse. Daisy had no choice but to allow her husband to have sex whenever he pleased. She could never tell him no, and she certainly could not claim rape because, as a wife slave, you do what your husband says or face disciplinary action, which in turn would be having to have forceful sex.

Wilheim was filthy rich, but he made his family live poor as he hid his funds from the household. The older Adolfi got, the more his hair began to get darker until finally, he had brown hair and was no longer considered a natural-born slave. As pleased as Adolfi was to no longer have to suffer what a natural-born slave must, the young boy still faced severe disciplinary action daily; While Adolfi tried to obey his father and grandfather, the child could not bear to disrespect his mother, his brother, Jakob, and little Anna. Adolfi certainly did not want to respect his oldest brother, Heinrich, but was led to believe that Heinrich was one of his superiors he must also obey. It made Adolfi jealous, in a sense, because Heinrich also was considered a natural-born slave, having red hair, but he was not treated like one as Adolfi had been.

Before becoming a teenager, Adolfi's mother grew very sick. Wilheim would not let her get the rest she needed as it did not matter that she was dying; she was still his slave. Jakob could not allow this to continue, so he gave up his room for his mother and kept a lock on the door to prevent his father from getting his way and killing her faster. Adolfi admired his brother's bravery. One day, while Jakob was out of the house running errands, he came home to see Wilheim trying to break down the door and get to Daisy. Jakob tried stopping him alone but needed help. Heinrich was not home as he was out following the German rule, not that he would have cared to help had he been home. Jakob could not ask Anna for help as she was still very young. So he called out for his brother, Adolfi, to help. In another room of the house, Adolfi could not ignore his brother's cries for help saving their dying mother.

Later, when Wilheim got Adolfi alone, he performed the worst form of discipline yet. He popped both of his son's eardrums, causing permanent deafness in both ears. After his mother had passed away, he now had to wear hearing aids so that he could hear to a certain extent. Adolfi, needing to learn to read lips, also suffered constant bullying by peers at school and even his family at home for being deaf. When asked how Adolfi lost his hearing, Wilheim said it was from listening to loud music to no end. That was when Adolfi decided it was time to join his father and all his superiors as they "avenge" their ancestors and take back what was rightfully theirs: America.

Adolfi knew he needed practice, so he chose his first victim, a neighborhood stray cat. As Adolfi played with his prey, the cat defended itself, clawing Adolfi's right arm so much that he lost feeling in the wounded area. The cat escaped, and Adolfi was left bleeding and needing medical attention. Later in life, Adolfi graduated high school with a bachelor's degree. Heinrich enslaved a woman,

Suzanna, whom he wed and had a son, Heinrich Jr. Jakob fell in love with his soon-to-be wife, Alana Brewski. Anna's father sold her to a man, Jonas Vogel. They wed and had a daughter, Audrey.

CHAPTER 3

Rosewitha's Struggles

In October 1961, Rosewitha was born to her mother, Orla, and her father, Ludwig Brewski. She was a sibling of eight, having two older brothers, Henry and Howie, and five older sisters—Eleven, Betty, Greta, Faith, and Alana. The children didn't see their father much as he was in the military. By the time Rosewitha turned two years old, Orla had gotten pregnant with another girl, Heidi, and during the pregnancy, Ludwig passed away. The family became very poor; the children would go to stores and steal clothing when they needed a fresh outfit. The older ones had to get jobs to help pay the bills since Orla's income alone was not nearly enough to support all nine children plus herself. Henry and Heidi were born disabled, having the mind of a child, so they needed more attention than the other siblings, who could take care of themselves when needed.

Rosewitha got along pretty well with all her siblings but had sibling rivalry with Greta and sometimes Alana. When Rosewitha was nine, she caught Alana smoking with a boyfriend and threatened to tell their mother. Alana threatened to beat Rosewitha if she did and convinced her younger sister to try a cigarette. Now that Rosewitha tried it, she would also get in trouble for smoking. Naturally, she became a smoker. In school, Rosewitha's best friend was Anna Averbach. Unfortunately, Rosewitha didn't graduate. She quit school to be able to afford things for herself and contribute to the household.

Howie became a truck driver and eventually met a woman, Beth, and they settled down and had two children, Cindy and Carl.

Eleven met a man, Jerry Zimmerman, and she unknowingly became his slave. While they were never married, they had three children, Jerry Jr. (JJ), Chrissy, and Catrina. Jerry's brother, Otto Zimmerman, enslaved Greta, married her, and they had twins. They named the girl Anja and the boy Otto Jr. (OJ). Betty became owned by a man, Wilheim Fuchs, whom she married and had two children with, Emma and Wilheim Jr. (Willy). Faith was fortunate to have met a true love, Jakob Miller, and they had four children, Noah, Daniel, Jennifer, and Sasha. While attending the William Floyd school district, Alana met her true love, Jakob Averbach. Unaware that his brother was part of a cult, Jakob mistakenly introduced Adolfi to Alana's sister, Rosewitha. Eventually, Jakob married Alana, and she became pregnant. But unfortunately for Jakob, he was not the father. Eleven's significant other had convinced Alana to have an affair with him, and now Jerry would have his fourth child, Raymond. It became agreed between the family that Raymond could not know who his biological father was although Alana had done the right thing and informed Jakob of him not being the father.

Adolfi then got Rosewitha pregnant and convinced her they must wed to have this child, claiming to be very religious. They got hitched at the town hall, having Jakob and Alana as their witnesses. Not long after, Alana became pregnant with her second child. This time, Jakob was the biological father. When the sonogram showed they would have a girl, they chose Ilse Leigh for the name. But when she delivered her beautiful new baby, it was a boy. Not having picked out a name for a boy, they named him after his father, Jakob Jr.

During this time, Rosewitha and Adolfi were having their second child. Adolfi prayed he would get his boy. His boy would be the perfect replica of himself; he would follow in his father's footsteps and avenge their ancestors. The sonogram showed a boy, and Adolfi chose the name Adam (after Adam and Eve) and Wilheim (after his father). Unknown to even the doctors, what they saw in the sonogram was not a penis as it must have been a finger, and since Adolfi and Rosewitha hadn't thought of a name for a girl, they just stole the name Alana had for the girl she thought she'd have.

CHAPTER 4

A Toddler's Supernatural Abilities

It was getting cold outside, and the holiday season was nearing. While Uncle Jerry and Aunt Eleven lived far away, they wouldn't come for the holidays, but before the day, they came out to visit the family. My grandmother owned a two-story home. When Otto enslaved my aunt, he also took ownership of my grandmother. Having only four rooms, two downstairs and two upstairs, my grandmother shared a room with Aunt Heidi. Uncle Henry had his room next to theirs while Otto and Aunt Greta shared a room upstairs, with Anja and OJ's room across from theirs.

At the family gathering, while all the kids were running upstairs to play in Anja and OJ's room, my mother made me nap in my grandma's room as she had coffee and hung out with the adults, so I laid on the bed trying to fall asleep when my cousin, Chrissy, slipped into my grandmother's room unnoticed and began kissing and licking my lips. Now I knew what everyone meant by wet kisses; I thought, I did not appreciate wet kisses at all. I didn't want to take a stupid nap, but while I had no choice, I just wanted her to let me sleep. Luckily, my mother was a worrywart and constantly checked on me even though she barricaded me with pillows and blankets for extra precaution, and she caught Chrissy and told her she couldn't be in the room where I was trying to sleep. That was when my cousin claimed to be only checking on me to be sure I was alright. My mother didn't mind her niece being protective, but she kindly asked Chrissy to get out anyway so I didn't wake up.

I pretended to stay asleep for a little while, but I heard more family coming over, which meant more kids to play with since I secretly hated Anja and OJ, and my sister was always mean to me when they were around. My father had always said they were both natural-born slaves, calling them redheaded stepchildren and saying he'd love to smack the freckles off of their bodies, so I didn't understand why they always thought they were the boss of me. I didn't act like their boss ever. I wanted them to treat me how I treated them. But Otto had them convinced they were not slaves, so they'd do what he said. Then as a reward, they'd get anything they wanted.

I was eager to play with my cousins, who had just arrived, so I called out for my mommy, who was there in the blink of an eye. Since there were too many kids to play in the room upstairs, we all went to play outside. There were so many kids that I lost track of who everyone was, forgetting even their names. They were running around, screaming and laughing, so I followed as best as possible, but that wasn't enough to keep up with them. While running and trying to catch up, my cousins and sister ran in the second entrance to my grandmother's basement. I was still near the first entryway when I heard a boy calling my name from inside. I knew it had to be one of my cousins since we were the only ones outside, so I put on a cheeky smile and ran toward the voice.

Inside stood one of my older cousins who was not even playing with us. All I could see was a taller male figure wearing pants and a flannel jacket, baring his penis for me to see as he called out, "Come here, come look." Not caring who it was, I screamed as loud as possible and ran out the door. My feet were now carrying me the fastest they ever had, and I ran into the second entrance to play with my cousins in that part of the basement. I began playing also, or trying to at least. OJ bitched that I was going to break his superexpensive train set. I wanted to tell someone what had just happened to me, but I couldn't even talk, and even if I could, I wasn't sure what did happen.

I tried to remember everyone who was at the house and also to remember who wore flannel jackets. I knew it could not be my uncle Henry as it wasn't even an adult. Plus, Uncle Henry was inside with the adults. And he loved me so much he would never do that to his niece or anyone. I remembered seeing Heinrich Jr. wear flannel jackets sometimes, but was he even at my grandma's? I could not recall no matter how hard I tried. But I knew one thing, Uncle Heinrich hated my grandma and everyone in her house, so I doubted it was his son. I couldn't recall ever seeing them there either.

As everyone was getting ready to leave Grandma's, I saw JJ as he put on his flannel jacket. When it was time to hug and kiss him goodbye, my insides felt strange. I didn't want to say goodbye to him or his sister and her wettest lips. They were both so kind to me though. I knew they loved me; they always said how funny and cute I was. I started feeling something different inside my body, guilt for even thinking they would ever even try to hurt their baby cousin. I thought about who else it could have been. I told myself it was Cousin Heinrich Jr., that stupid redheaded stepchild. Now whenever I would have to go to see him, I would have to keep my eye on him; I was not going to let that stupid German hurt me or anyone I loved. But if Daddy could pretend to love my uncle Heinrich, I could do the same to Heinrich Jr. I didn't see him often since our fathers stopped speaking, so I figured I should be able to do it.

When we left Grandma's and got back home, I went straight to my playroom/sister's room, grabbed my favorite toy for one hand and my least favorite for the other hand, and I declared WW3. I wanted to play with all my toys and have a real war, but when my father was home, his children could only play with two toys, one for each hand. If they wanted to play with other toys, the ones they held had to get put away.

Later, at bedtime, I felt so sick that I couldn't sleep. That was when I heard my father tell my mother to take her underwear off. Knowing what that meant, I lay in my crib as tears rolled down my face and onto my pillow as I tried to stay quiet so that no one would know I was still awake. When I finally fell asleep, I dreamed I was in my car seat with my sister sitting next to me while our father was driving and our mother was in the passenger seat. We then pulled into the parking lot of the small building where my parents would go once a month to pay car insurance. As the building was small, so was the parking lot. Since my father always made his children wait outside in the locked car, he did the same in my dream. This time, I didn't mind as much because I didn't have to hear him say, "Keep the doors locked because there are lots of serial killers out here and they will snatch you girls right up." Instead, I heard my sister say, "Let's play in the parking lot since it's empty, and if a car comes, we'll run back into our car." I loved the sound of that, and my sister unbuckled me so that I could climb out of my car seat.

While we were running in a circular position, a brown station wagon pulled up, and I looked at my sister's scared face as she yelled, "Let's go in the building by Mommy!" I tried following her, but I was stuck running in the circle and couldn't stop as I watched her run inside, not even looking back for me. When I tried calling my sister, I suddenly realized I had no voice when trying to call out "Sissy!"

A lady with long, brown, wavy hair parked the brown station wagon in the parking spot farthest from my parents' car, a light-blue Oldsmobile cutlass. This lady reminded me of my aunt Greta although my aunt had a round belly while this lady was skinny. My aunt also had flat, pin-straight brown hair, and her station wagon was white with a thin brown line on either side of the car from the front to the back. The lady walked over to me, gently grabbed my arm, breaking the circular motion I was stuck in, and walked me to her vehicle. As she opened the back driver's side door, I saw an empty car seat, and she picked me up and put me in. While she buckled me in, she introduced me to her son. He was sitting in his car seat on the back passenger side. He had reddish-brown curly hair and freckles covering his face, neck, and arms, which reminded me of my cousin, OJ.

As the lady pulled out of her spot and drove away, I watched the door, hoping my parents would come out to save me. Once I could no longer see the familiar building where my parents were, my hopes and dreams of being saved were just that. The lady pulled into an empty dirt lot, except for a kid's ride-on motorbike, and took her son out of his car seat, placing him on the bike. Then she walked back to the car for me and sat me on the bike behind her son. Saying goodbye, she told me to hold her son tight so I do not fall off and get hurt. Once she pulled out of the dirt lot, the boy drove the bike to the road, following the same way his mother had driven, and not long after, we pulled up to a brown house where the brown station wagon was in the driveway. He parked the motorbike right behind his mother's vehicle, and we went inside, where plates of spaghetti and meat sauce were on the dining room table.

As the three of us sat to eat, the boy had no manners, and he ate like a disgusting pig, getting sauce and small pieces of spaghetti stuck to his face, neck, and shirt. I thought of how if my father saw this he would probably scream at the boy for being so disgusting when he ate. Once we finished eating, the lady disappeared into the kitchen and returned with Oreo cookies and milk for dessert. She didn't even bother to clean her son's face from dinner before he started chowing down as if he had never eaten before, leaving him to add cookies and milk to the mess he made of himself. I thought, *If I ever ate that way, my father would beat me with a belt.*

Once we finished dessert, his mother directed us to the bathroom where she had started a shower and kindly demanded I take a shower with her son. We had to clean each other off and then we had to kiss under the running water while his mother took pictures with her camera. Relieved when it was finally over, I got good news from the lady. She informed me that I could now call my mother and have her pick me up as she handed me her phone and dialed the number for me.

By the time I awoke from this dreadful nightmare of a dream, I had now been on the couch in the living room with my mother, rocking me while she held me close and said, "It's alright, my baby. It was probably just a bad dream. Mommy's here for you. You are safe."

Knowing my mother was right, I held her tight and fell asleep in the only safe place I knew I had: my mother's loving arms. Little did either my mother or I know, it wasn't just a bad dream but a premonition of what would become my reality soon.

CHAPTER 5

All I Want After Christmas

My birthday passed, and I was two years old, another year closer to fighting for world peace. I got presents from my parents on my birthday, and we had cake. The following week, it was Christmas. I was excited to open my presents and to see what presents my sister would get. My favorite toy was my new green-and-yellow Glo Worm. Ada got the same toy, but her Glo Worm was purple and pink. I was a little sad because I liked her Glo Worm colors better than mine, but I got over it knowing that once school was back in session, I would play with it until it was time to pick her up. Plus, my sister played with me where she would hold her worm and I would have mine. Ada didn't know it, but my worm told her worm we would be going to WW3, and her worm said okay.

Not long after the holiday season, my mother noticed that my four front teeth were beginning to turn a dark color, so she brought me to the dentist. There, I got to play with toys while we waited to get called into the patient room. I loved the dentist's office; it was great. After being seen, the receptionist gave me a sticker and a lollipop; it was so awesome! When we got home, my mother told my father that she had to make another appointment to get my four front teeth pulled so it wouldn't ruin my adult teeth. I thought Daddy was going to baby me like he usually did, but instead, he got upset for having to take me to the dentist for the second time in the year. Once he wasn't angry over that anymore and my mother wasn't around to hear, he told me that when I go, they will put a mask on me that makes me fall asleep, and I have to be careful not to swallow my teeth or I could choke and die. I no longer wanted to go there again, but on the day of my appointment, my mother put me in my car seat, and we drove to that dreadful place. When they called my name, I thought my heart would pop out of my chest. I heard the dentist and my mom whispering that once I fell asleep from the laughing gas, she would bring my sister back into the waiting room so that they weren't in the way and Ada could play instead of sitting and having nothing to do.

The dentist agreed it would be alright to leave because I'd be sleeping and wouldn't even know they were gone. I no longer liked my dentist, and I closed my eyes and passed right out. I had a dream where my teeth got sucked into the mask and they floated around, getting near my mouth. Afraid, I thought I would swallow one or even all of them. I was screaming so loud for my mother that it woke me up, so the assistant told me she would get her for me. I was relieved once she immediately came to me, but I still couldn't stop crying, and now I also wanted my grandma. I cried out for her, not realizing that Grandma didn't even go with us. My mother took my sister and me straight to my grandmother's, and it warmed my heart to know that she would do anything to take my fears away. As my mother became that way because her mother did the same for her, naturally, I would need that extra love and nurture from my mother after such a traumatizing event.

As I had all the love and nurturing I needed to heal myself from not only my grandmother and my mother but also my aunt Heidi and uncle Henry when they returned home from their jobs at a company that hired special people to work, making a penny per piece of something they made, I was so excited to be waiting at their bus stop, right outside my grandmother's house, with my mother and also my sister. My aunt and uncle were always just as excited as my sister and I, and we'd share a special welcome-home moment since it wasn't an everyday thing, only if we were visiting Grandma upon their arrival. Today felt even more special as it was like a get-well-soon moment. Not everyone who lived there was so emotionally loving and caring though.

Aunt Greta said I was acting like a baby; it didn't even hurt, and it was what I got for drinking too much soda. Her children ate and drank worse things than I was allowed to, so I felt she shouldn't be talking. Whenever my cousins would bully me around, Anja was never as ruthless as OJ, but they would not stop picking on me and always got my sister to join them. They all ran over to me as I sat on my grandmother's lap, and OJ told me to smile so they could see what it looked like. Once I did, they all ran away screaming, and they seemed so silly that it made me laugh. Then they came over, and OJ said to smile again. Thinking it was a game, I smiled big, and while Anja and Ada did as they did the first time, just screamed and ran away, OJ yelled out that I looked ugly. It hurt my feelings a little, but right after he had, my grandmother and mother both yelled at him, saying that wasn't nice. As my grandmother, mother, aunt Heidi, and uncle Henry were saying how adorable I looked, Aunt Greta started defending OJ's actions by "again" telling me that this was what I got for drinking too much soda.

    I could tell my mother was getting tired of her sister's mouth and the kids teasing me, all while I was not feeling well because she told my grandmother that we had to leave after she finished her cup of coffee. My mother would always have at least two cups of coffee, sometimes three, depending on the length of our visit, and she only had one cup thus far. As much as I loved being at my grandmother's for the ones who loved and respected me, I couldn't wait to get away from the ones for who I could feel their hatred and resentment toward me as their jealousy was visible.

    Back at home was peaceful. I got to go to Joseph and Lynette's part of our white castle and show them what had happened to me where I was, again, loved and nurtured some more. And when my father got home, he babied me for a little bit. It didn't last too long as things turned in the opposite direction. He began singing a Christmas song, "All I want for Christmas is my four front teeth." I was so tired of getting picked on and having such a long day. I couldn't help but let some tears out, so my mother asked him to stop it because he was upsetting me and I needed to rest. He laughed it off and told my sister to join in, so she did, and they both kept singing the song. When I couldn't take it anymore and more tears ran down my face than before, my father told me that I needed to learn how to take a fucking joke, and if I wanted to cry, he'd give me something to be crying about.

I immediately managed to stop the tears from forming as my mother defended my right to be upset. I appreciated that she did, but at the same time, I wished she hadn't. Now, my parents were fighting; my father was insinuating my mother wanted her daughters to be big-titty babies and cry over everything as she does, and I just wanted this day to be over. I felt so tired and drained from my big day that the arguing made me feel worse. It was my fault that my mother was getting treated like a slave because I just couldn't take a fucking joke. Upon worrying that my father would later be making my mother have sex with him that night, I felt so drained that as soon as my mother laid me down and tucked me in, I fell into a deep sleep. When thinking that everyone would move on and stop teasing me, it only got worse as my father now had Anja and Otto singing his version of the Christmas song to me, and I couldn't wait for my teeth to grow in so that they would stop. I found it even more annoying since it wasn't Christmastime anymore, and Christmas music only played on the radio before and during Christmas.

CHAPTER 6

Bitches Get Burned at Any Age

Between constantly being picked on about losing my teeth, the abuse I suffered when I was not obeying my father and our fathers before him, and all the horrible things my family was telling me, like that people would be getting killed by poisons put in their cigarettes, I just could not take it anymore. I wanted to die, so I decided that I was going to start being a smoker like my mother. When she wasn't looking around her pack of cigarettes, I grabbed her lighter and a cigarette and ran underneath the table. My mother didn't use just any lighter; she had a Zippo, which took me a little bit to remember how Mommy does it. My sister noticed that she didn't see me for a while, so she assumed I was playing hide-and-seek, and she went searching for me.

With a big smile, my sister peeked under the table and said, "Found you." Seeing that I had a cigarette in my mouth and the lighter in my hand, still trying to figure out how to ignite it, my sister cried out, "Mommy, Ilse's under the table trying to smoke!"

Our mother gave me a huge lecture about how cigarettes were a nasty and disgusting habit that was hard to break. I already knew that; every smoker in my family stunk, especially their breath when they'd kiss me. I wanted to get cancer and die so I wouldn't have to feel the pain I felt for all the slaves I know and don't know, slaves still alive, and those who were dead, as well as the pain I had for myself.

It took a toll on me, so I wanted to be with the dead slaves. At least then I could meet my grandma Daisy.

I was deeply saddened by what life was like, but something that always brought up my spirits was listening to Mommy's music. One day, my father was farting around and had yet to put in his hearing aids while my mother was doing laundry. As she was folding clothes and listening to my favorite black singer, Michael Jackson, I was dancing and trying to sing along when my father saw the record cover. I figured, "Eh, he can't hear, so he has no clue that's what I'm dancing to." I didn't realize that he didn't have to have hearing aids in his ears to know what was playing, and he came to his bedroom, put in his hearing aids, and asked that I follow him into the kitchen, claiming he wanted to tell me something important.

My mother had made a pot of coffee before going to fold clothes. My father saw the cord plugged into the outlet, and he got cranky because in our house, as soon as you finish using something, it had to get unplugged. He ripped out the cord, leaving it to hang over the counter, which my mother would never do for our safety, knowing coffee was very hot. We sat at the table, and he started talking to me about the Bible and how I must never listen to n—— like that or I will have to get disciplined; he said how I was born with the choice of if I want to be rich and successful like him and his side of the family or a poor slut slave like my mother and her side of the family. My father explained that if he saw I was following the wrong path instead of the "true" way he followed, he would have to be sure I turned around and followed him again.

I didn't want to follow his path; it wasn't true at all, and I could not understand why he didn't see this. I looked at the coffeepot and pointed to show him that the cord was hanging, and he responded with "Yeah, yeah, yeah, never mind that right now, it's not important, ignore it for now," and he continued with his lecture. I then tried to communicate and show him what my eyes could see, thinking maybe my brain could get to his brain somehow, but I wound up getting lost and came across a carefree place where no one could hurt me. That was when my father yelled at me for daydreaming instead of paying attention to "important" life lessons, and he called me stupid.

As thankful as I was that he finally stopped talking, I was unaware of his intentions for my form of discipline. He began to walk out of the kitchen but turned to me and said, "Hey, kitten, can you do your dear old dad a favor and push that plug up so no one gets hurt?"

I thought this was my chance to show him that I obey him when it's to do good things, so I proudly walked over and tried to push it up, but I was too short. I heard my father say to give it slack, and knowing what that meant from being taught with his ropes, I pulled the cord back so I could throw it better. The coffeepot fell over, pouring scorching hot coffee over my left shoulder, immediately burning my skin. I tried to scream, but nothing came out, just like in my dream, and I looked over to find that my father had already left the kitchen. I ran to my mother's room, who was finishing the laundry, and there my father was lying on the bed as if everything was fine. He saw me moving weirdly and tears rolling down my face, but instead of helping me, he told my mother, "Rosewitha, look how cute. Ilse's dancing like a monkey."

My mother looked, and at first glance, she started to smile and said "Aww" until she noticed I was not dancing and laughing; I was crying in pain. That's when she saw the coffee on my clothes and called an ambulance. She tried taking my wet clothes off, but I screamed louder than I ever could, and she decided it was best to wait for the ambulance to arrive. While we waited, she held me close, telling me I would be okay as she was also crying.

As if I hadn't felt ugly enough between losing my four front teeth and getting teased for it, I had to have my long hair chopped off like a boy so that hair wouldn't touch the third-degree burn wound. The back of my shoulder was now an ugly wrinkly bubble, and I was not allowed to bathe for three weeks, sponge baths only. I hated going to Grandma's because all the adults and kids kept wanting to see it, and someone would always feel the need to say "Wow, that's an ugly burn" or "That's gonna be one ugly scar." I'd have to hear how I look like a boy with my hair chopped off, and some would say how now I did look like an Adam Wilheim. And, of course, OJ kept making fun of me for it. I wished my mother would stop moving my shirt to let people see the healing process. I knew some people like my grandmother were concerned, but it was embarrassing and made me want to die since I was such a hideous monster.

One day, out on my grandmother's porch, my mother wanted to show Aunt Greta how it was healing so well, and she went to move my shirt over to show my scar. I broke free from her, ran over to the brick pillar, and slammed my forehead so hard that I saw nothing but black and some stars. I heard my aunt ask my mother if she saw what I just did, and my mother replied, "Yup, and I bet she won't do that again." Even though I was crying since that hurt, I thought, *Yup, I will do it again, just not on bricks.* I couldn't understand why, but the pain I felt after banging my head felt great. My brain felt clear even though I had a pounding headache and a huge knot on my forehead. It didn't bother me that Anja, OJ, and my sister were now laughing, saying I looked like a unicorn. And when no one was looking, I would push on it, and I felt that great jolt through my whole body again as it did when I first got hurt.

It was getting very tiring, and I was becoming irritable with having to listen to my panicked mother remind me how now that the sun was getting stronger, I could not be in it too long and I had to wear sunblock. She'd tell me how important it was to listen to the doctor because the doctor said I could get skin poisoning or it could become cancerous. My hatred for my father's side of the family grew stronger and stronger each time I had to hear him remind me that had I not listened to that n—— music, he wouldn't have had to discipline me and I would have never gotten burned. I didn't know how else to handle the situation but to cause my mother and sister extreme stress by being spiteful and not listening.

The more my father heard that I had misbehaved, the more he praised me for obeying. He didn't know that was not my intention. I was trying to express my emotions, and everyone had their way of doing that, so I didn't know how to express them other than to act out. No one could hear my screams inside saying, *Enough, listen to me!*

CHAPTER 7

Goodbye, White Castle

One night, while my father had gone out to do "whatever it was" he did, my sister and I were playing with our toys in the living room when we saw a bug crawling around on our coffee table. Ada wanted to play with it, and she started poking at it. Then I burst into laughter because the bug was freaking out, trying to get away from her, but she just would not let it escape as she kept poking it with every turn the bug tried making to free itself. My mother wanted to see what was making me so giggly, and once she saw what my sister had been doing, she screamed, "Oh, fuck, Ada, stop that! Icky, that's a cockroach!"

She pulled my sister off the coffee table and took us downstairs to let our landlord know we had roaches. I loved visiting them. I sat on Lynette's lap and tried to tell her that I wished I could live with her in her part of the white castle, but she didn't really understand me and just hugged me, saying how cute she thought I was. She never once made fun of me for missing my four front teeth, for getting burned, or when my hair got chopped off, causing me to look like a boy. I loved her and Joseph so much and never wanted to leave our white castle. I was going to get older and be able to tell them everything, and they were going to join me as I stopped the evil Germans and made them go back to their own fucking country.

When my father returned from work, my mother informed him of the bug problem. Right away, he started to yell at her, telling her if she didn't sit on her ass drinking coffee all day and gossiping with her family, we wouldn't have roaches. She told my father it was not just upstairs, downstairs had them too. My father then blamed our landlord, accusing them of being filthy fucking slobs and told my mother we had to start looking for a new place to live. Having heard what my father said, I became upset, thinking, *I could not leave my white castle.* Unfortunately, I didn't have a say, and my father found a stupid one-story red house that looked like an ugly barn.

While visiting my favorite Indian man, Barry, he made me feel so much better about everything that I had gone through since we last saw him. Barry was so proud of me that I could talk more, and I wanted to make him more proud by calling out his name, "Bowie." Everyone laughed and said "Aww," but my father had to correct me, "It's Barry, Kit, not Bowie."

Barry interrupted my father respectfully and said I could call him Bowie if I wanted to. Then my dear friend Bowie said something like music to my ears, "Once you get a little older, I can start teaching you about your Indian heritage."

My father pretended to be so excited about it, claiming he'd like to learn himself that he even had me fooled. My heart felt the warmest it had in a while; this beautiful sunny day became more like heaven on Earth and less like hell. That was until we got in the car to go home. My father showed me his true colors again and bitched the whole ride about how I will not be learning about my Indian heritage. He yelled at me to forget that I am Indian, saying I'm not even a real Indian anyway, so if I tell people I am, I will sound stupid.

My father left me no choice but to go to that place I found in my head. A place where no one could hear me and no one could hurt me. In there, I called my father everything that I could remember hearing my mother call him, mixed with things he said to me, "You fucking stupid deaf bastard, why can't you see that you are following the wrong path? Don't you want to go to a paradise island where all of humankind, not just mankind, will be able to live without worry and carefree, a place where you can pet lions and tigers and bears? Oh my. Or are you that fucking stupid that you just want to go to hell where you will never rest in peace and your sins will haunt you for all eternity?"

Before I knew it, we were on our block, and our white castle, which would soon no longer be ours, was awaiting the entrance of its princess, me.

On the day we were moving out of the white castle, my mother snuck in and let us say goodbye to Joseph and Lynette before my father returned to get us and bring us to the new place. As much as I loved my family, I wished I could be their daughter instead. It was heartbreaking to know that I may never see them again. I thought how sad the white castle would be without its princess. I remembered how I always thought of myself as Rapunzel and my father was the evil trapping me in the tower. That memory brought up the reality that I no longer heard people call me Rapunzel and tell me to let down my long hair since my hair got chopped off, and now I looked like Adam Wilheim.

I became sad and thought, *Who am I kidding? I'm no princess anyway. My father's side of the family is just stupid and thinks they are royalty when they aren't.*

And when we were leaving the white castle, as my father said "Good riddance," I was thinking, *I will never forget you, white castle, or you, Joseph, Lynette, and Rebecca.*

CHAPTER 8

New People with New Surroundings

After moving into our new home at 281 Darkened Circle in Mystic Bay, my father brought me to see the landlord for something. When we arrived, I saw an old man, and my father told me, "That's Antony, our landlord." Then pointing to a young black boy who stood near our landlord, my father said, "That's a slave."

He was annoyed that our landlord would dare bring his slave to a meeting where I would be. I learned later that this boy was our landlord's grandson, and I was so confused because my father had changed his tone in another direction and smiled and said hi to both the landlord and his grandson. The boy, Frances, was ready and willing to play as I tried to please my father and pretended I was not interested in playing, only to be confused when my father said it was alright to play with him. Knowing my father, this might have been a test, so I socialized cautiously. After my father and the landlord finished talking and were saying their goodbyes, I ran to our car without saying goodbye to Frances as I wished I could call him my friend. When we got in the car and left, my father teased that poor innocent child, and although it offended me, I pretended to agree with my dear old dad.

The first neighbor we met was the family in the house to our left, a man, who was also named Adolfi, his wife, Rosa, and their son, David. My mother and Rosa found it quite amusing that they had very similar names and that their husbands had the same name. They felt they were "destined" to meet and immediately became friends. David was older than me but younger than my sister. I was happy to have someone to play with, but David and my sister knew how to play with things that I didn't, so I would go off and play with their family pet, a cat named Sandra. She immediately caught my attention, a playful black-and-white kitty. So while the adults talked and David and my sister played his toys and games, I'd sit near my mother and Rose, and Sandra would come right to me, loving me, kneading me, and purred and headbutted me if I stopped petting her even for a second. The sounds of the cat's purr and the echoes of my mother and Rosa's laughter were so beautiful; I felt like I had been floating on a cloud, but I hated when I heard the footsteps of the two Adolfis coming upstairs from the basement. That sound always made me feel like someone grabbed onto the cloud I was sitting on and pulled it down as my happiness became sadness as it meant my father would say it was time to go back home. That's when my father would begin his routine of shit talking.

He'd call Rosa a slut and David a retard, and he would speak highly of Adolfi. When I was alone with my father, he would tell me that Rosa and David were Adolfi's slaves. I would let him "go on and on" as I allowed myself to drift away into my secret hideaway in my mind. I listened to the peaceful sound of my mother and Rosa cracking up; I'd hear Sandra purring. Then farther in the background, I could hear distant sounds of my sister and David having fun yet sometimes not agreeing on things. I was able to listen to all this while also hearing my father's tone of voice to know if he was questioning me so that I could answer his question. This way, I wouldn't get called stupid for daydreaming.

The second family we met was in the house across the street from us, Joe and his wife, Jessica, and their dog, Sweety. Sweety was a beautiful all-black long-haired dog that loved to play with running hose water. My father fell in love with Sweety and wanted a dog like her. Joe and Jessica were pretty wealthy and had a lot of expensive stuff, and my father would pretend to be interested in it, which led to Joe talking about things like where he got it, how much it cost, etc. My favorite part of their house was the backyard. I loved going into

Sweety's doghouse, and I enjoyed the rides Joe would give my sister and me on his ride-on lawn mower. It was always so much fun until it was time to leave.

My dear old dad would start mocking our new friends. "Hi, I'm Jessica, and I'm a slut. Hi, I'm Joe, and I think I'm better than everyone because I work for an electric company and I'm filthy rich." If he saw that I wasn't laughing along with his insults, he'd call me stupid and accuse me of daydreaming again as if anything he said about them was funny.

David was friends with his neighbor to the left side of his house. In that home was a man, Marc, his wife, Mandy, and their son, Marc Jr. Mandy had been pregnant at the time and was the biggest bitch while her husband thought he was the best thing in the world. As for Marc Jr., the rotten apple didn't fall too far from the tree.

My family didn't associate with them much, except when David and Marc Jr. would play at David's house. My sister and I would be courteous and treat him the way we would want him to treat us. Although if he'd piss me off, which he did a lot, I will let my brain do all the talking, *You are the retard, not David. You are so ugly and stupid, and, ooh, I really cannot stand you, you fucking piece of shit.*

Marc Jr. was the kind who thought he was better than everyone because his parents made good money, and he didn't shy away from trying to make the less fortunate feel bad about themselves. It didn't work on me as I was humble and appreciated the little things in life. It only made me wish I could send him and his family back to where they came from, being unborn.

To the right of my house was a brown house with a beautiful brown family. I saw a man, a woman, a boy who looked older than my sister, and a girl that seemed to be my age. I knew that my father always warned me that "I was always watched" and that my life was like the story that Fred Savage reads in *The Princess Bride*, but somehow I was going to make that girl my best friend, and her family was going to join my army.

I knew I had plenty of opportunities to make friends with the neighbors, who I was supposed to hate, being my father worked full-time and sometimes went to the city, and he also loved going out for walks alone. One day, my mother took my sister and me to the backyard to play. The girl and her mother were outside in their backyard, so I asked my mother if we could say hi to them. My mother waved, and the neighbor waved back, eventually leading us toward the gate that separated our yards while we all introduced ourselves. The girl's name was Imani. She was so pretty and funny, and I immediately loved my best friend.

As my mother was aware of her husband's racist ways, she let Imani's mother know about it, explaining he was that way because of his father being a racist and how when he would be home, I wouldn't be allowed to play with Imani. She understood and made my mother aware that she has no issues with us being friends and that she respects my father's rules. She appreciated my mother's honesty and didn't want me to get in trouble. Imani told me her brother's name was Pokey. I loved that name; it reminded me of Gumby and Pokey, and I couldn't wait to meet him. He looked old enough to join my army, so I wanted to let him and his parents know my plan. I didn't want to allow Imani to join my army; she would have to stay safe with my mom and sister while we went to World War 3, and I was sure her parents and her brother would agree with me.

CHAPTER 9

White Tiperella

One day, while my father and Adolfi were chatting near the gate, I asked if I could bring Sandra to my room in my house, and he said yes and gave her to my father to pass to me. I held her carefully while I ran to the back door and into my house. Once we got inside, I gave her a quick tour and brought her to my room, showing her all my favorite toys and explaining they were my practice army people. Then I showed her which toys were the evil Germans and gave her the Andy doll I got from my great-aunt Bertha. She gave me Andy because Andy represents Adam, and she gave my sister Raggedy Ann because she represents Eve. Great-Aunt Bertha said that was why it's called Raggedy Ann and Andy.

I let Sandra play and attack Andy, and then she knocked it over by my play shopping basket. The silly kitty got curious, smelling the basket, and stepped inside, so I put my face near her and asked, "We go store." The cat started to purr and pushed her nose into my lips, so I happily grabbed the handles, picked up the basket, and pretended to be taking her shopping. Suddenly, Sandra's foot fell into one of the holes in the basket, and the scared kitty started freaking out, crying, screeching, and trying to climb up me in hopes that it would free her. She accidentally scratched me up a little bit, but I didn't care; I just wanted to help her, and since pulling her foot out wasn't possible, I ran outside to get the grown-ups. I couldn't help but cry because I was so afraid she was hurt, and I had Adolfi and my father come to me so I could show them what was happening to poor Sandra.

They quickly ran to my room, and Adolfi attended to his pet while my father was angry, seeing that the cat had clawed me up. He kept saying I was hurt or that she hurt me, and I kept shaking my head, saying, "No, kitty hurt." He would not listen to me. Once Adolfi got Sandra's foot unstuck, he came to me to make sure I was okay, and he explained that Sandra loved me, but she was just scared.

I asked him, "Is she hurt?"

He said she was fine, and I did the right thing by coming to get him because Sandra could've seriously hurt me. No one understood me when I said I was not hurt. I felt something "amazing" that I could not control. I enjoyed getting cut; I loved the pain more than when I banged my head or pushed on bruises.

A couple of days passed, and my mother went to the front door to find a cat's tail in the street outside of our yard. Worried, she told my father to check it out because it looked like Sandra's tail. He went outside to pick it up and bring it to Rosa's. The whole time he was gone, I was praying that she was alright, and when he returned, my father told us that it was Sandra's tail. She didn't come inside the night before when Rosa tried calling her, but she was at the door in the early morning, crying to be let in and having a bloody stub for a tail. My father claimed it must have been a raccoon and then told us, "Serves her right. That raccoon gave her what she deserved for cutting up my little princess. That slut cat is lucky he let her off easy."

I was glad Sandra was still alive and well, but I was so upset because I felt it was my fault she didn't want to go home, and then the poor kitty got attacked by a raccoon. Later, my mother took my sister and me to Rosa's so I could see that Sandra was, in fact, okay. I couldn't shake the feeling my father was lying to me and thought she might be dead, but when we got to Rosa's, I saw her alive and scared. Sandra didn't want to love me as usual, but Rosa said to give her time and Sandra would be her old self again. Soon enough, she was, and she was so cute, wagging her little nubby stub when I made her happy.

Seeing how Sandra losing a tail had affected me, my father felt guilty and wanted to make it up to his baby girl. As cruel as my father was, he sometimes had a soft spot where he would do almost anything to see me smile again. One day, he brought home a kitten, a beautiful black-and-white kitty, all my own. She was so tiny compared to Sandra and more playful. My father named her White Tiperella as her tail was all black until the tip was white. I loved the name because it was similar to Cinderella, one of my favorite Disney princesses. She loved hiding under the couch, and when I'd run past, she'd run up and cling to the back of my leg and bite me. My father showed me how to cut up with her. You dig into their belly, and they attack you; push on their rabbitlike feet, and they will kick and bite you; and it's just the cutest thing ever.

White Tiperella was so funny when my father would read the newspaper. He would go over and sit in his recliner, and White Tiperella would jump onto his shoulder. If his head was facing the left of the paper, so was hers. When he would turn his head to the right, so did she. As he would turn the page, she would tap on the page as if she was helping him, and she would spin her head in a circular motion while my father flipped to the next page. But poor White Tiperella was not excluded from beatings when my father felt it was necessary to teach her a lesson for doing things like scratching the furniture or if I'd let her cut up with me and if she'd accidentally scratch me or other catlike things she did since she was a cat and it was natural to her. He would grab her by the back of her neck and wail on her rear end hard as my kitty would yelp in pain and try to get away from the beating. After beating her so many times, my father would forcefully throw her across the room; most times, White Tiperella landed on her feet and ran to find a safe place to hide, but sometimes, her tiny body would slam into the wall before she landed on her feet.

CHAPTER 10

Aunt Elephant

At the age of two and a half, I could speak considerably well since I had practiced over and over every chance I got. My uncle Howie was visiting, and I could almost say his full respective name. It was a short visit since he was only stopping through while on a journey for his work. Uncle Howie never had time to stop at each family member's house but would stop at my grandma's, and if you wanted to see him, you'd know the date and time of his arrival and where to go for the visit.

For this visit, my mother had taken us to my grandmother's early so we could greet him when he arrived as she let us do for Aunt Heidi and Uncle Henry. When Uncle Howie pulled up, Ada was upstairs playing with Anja and OJ, and I was outside with my mother while she was smoking a cigarette. I could see how happy my uncle was to see me as he parked his eighteen-wheeler out front. He exited the truck, and we ran to each other as my mother cried out, "Ilse, please slow down so you don't trip over your own feet."

I jumped into my uncle's arms, and we spun around as we hugged and kissed. It had been a while since we last saw each other, definitely not since I had gotten burned and had my hair chopped off, and I could feel the energy of my uncle's love and sympathy for me. My eyes teared up, and I started to cry.

He looked at me and asked, "Would you like to see the inside of my big truck?"

I stopped crying immediately and smiled so big. "Yes!"

My mother was worried I might fall trying to get in, so Uncle Howie got in the driver's seat while my mother stood behind me on the passenger side, giving me a boost as I climbed in; my uncle held out his hand for me to grab so he could pull me in. Once the three of us were inside the truck, my mother and uncle were catching up when we saw Ada, Anja, and OJ running out of the house to see Uncle Howie. Knowing how careless and disrespectful Anja and OJ were, my uncle had informed my mother that if it were just Ada, he'd let her in his truck because he knew she was respectful and cautious like me; with the other two coming, he kindly asked mommy to help him help me out, and we got out of the truck. I felt bad that my sister couldn't go in, but I enjoyed hearing Anja and OJ get all upset and say how unfair it was that I got to go inside.

After we went inside the house, other family members began arriving, and OJ kept teasing me for being Uncle Howie's favorite out of all his nieces and nephews as if that would have hurt my feelings, and he kept trying to get our cousins to join in. But even when they had, like Cousin Sasha, I just smiled because I loved hearing over and over again how I was the one our uncle had the strongest bond with. It wasn't that he didn't love all his nieces and nephews because he sure did, and he also knew that every time something traumatic happened to me, some of my cousins and my sister constantly made fun of me for it. Uncle Howie knew how Anja and OJ treated everyone without being told. When he'd call his mother's house every single time, he'd hear OJ cursing her out to get him what he wanted or misbehaving in another way, and while Anja didn't speak to our grandma the way her brother did, she was still very disrespectful to her. When my uncle called my mother, my sister and I were the complete opposite and only did typical kid things. And that was how it was when he'd call his other sisters' houses. The kids were respectful for the most part. I always had to know who my mother was on the phone with in case it was my uncle Howie because I never wanted to miss talking to him, so I would annoy my mother until she finally yelled at me as she told me who was on the phone. When it was Uncle Howie, she'd hand me the phone, and my uncle would say it's great to talk to me, but I should be more respectful to Mommy and wait my turn. He promised he would never hang up the call unless he got to speak to me.

While all the Brewski siblings looked alike, the one who looked most like Uncle Howie was my aunt Eleven. The fact that they both lived far away and I barely ever got to see them made my heart grow fonder for her as it did him. Whenever Uncle Howie came out to visit, Aunt Eleven hadn't, and vice versa, so when one was visiting, they filled the void of not having the other. This time when it was Aunt Eleven who was coming for a visit, I found out we were going to the park. I was so excited because not only was I going to see my aunt and cousins, but also I got to visit all the lost loved ones that I never got to meet, the ones who my family and other Germans hid their bodies after killing them for not obeying.

Knowing my aunt was enslaved by her "better" half, I wanted to do something special for her. I could already kind of say her name as I called her "Aunt Evy," but I wanted to try to pronounce her full name because I knew it would make her so happy. When she asked me to come and sit on her lap, I walked over with a big smile and climbed up. I looked at her and proudly said "Aunt Elephant." Everyone began laughing, and my aunt loved it so much that she had tears rolling down her cheeks as she asked me to repeat it, so I did. The laughter had been just as loud as the first time I said it.

Knowing that even the evilest relative has suffered such horrifying traumas, it was important to me to do my best to make my family happy and have a good time, especially on such a beautiful day. I wished it could stay this way and the whole world would stop being so mean to everyone. I wanted everyone to know that I know their pain and how sorry I am for them, how if I could have taken their beatings, I would have because no one deserves abuse in any way, shape, or form. And when the time came for my precious aunt to return to her dreadful home, I felt an emptiness taking over inside me, not knowing when I would be able to see her or my uncle Howie again.

CHAPTER 11

The Test at Dr. Schultz's Office

Diagonally across the street from my grandmother's house, Anja's friend's dog had a litter of puppies. My father felt overly guilty for how he had been treating his precious princess and said maybe we could take one of the puppies home. I was so excited to hear that and even more excited when he said I would be allowed to pick the puppy. He got into a lecture about how I must obey the rules so I could have anything and everything I possibly wanted. He informed me that he would be testing my obedience before he could make a decision. He added that I would not know where or when, but if I passed the test, I would get rewarded. I didn't care to listen to his boring lecture, so I disappeared into the safe place in my head and imagined the day we would get to bring our new puppy home. I already knew which one I would be picking.

While most of the litter looked like their mother, one puppy stood out; it was the only gray puppy with a bit of white on her paws and chest and the tip of her tail, just like my kitty, White Tiperella. I wondered where the puppy's father was and if she looked like her daddy as I looked like mine. I thought about how sad the puppy would be when we took her away from her mommy and siblings, and then I got sick to my stomach, thinking of how I'd feel if I got taken from my family. I quickly thought of ways to cheer the puppy up when she missed her family. When my father realized I was daydreaming, he told me to cut that out, and if I didn't pass the test given to me, I would not even get the puppy. Then he reminded me that I would not know I was being tested, and not only would I not get a puppy, but I'd have to get disciplined for failing as well.

The schools would be back in session soon, so my sister had to go to the doctor. At her appointment, my father demanded I wait with him in the waiting room while my mother went into the patient room with my sister. I didn't know why he even came to this appointment; he never cared to attend any of Ada's doctor visits. Then as a friendly colored boy approached me, asking if I wanted to play with him, I figured this was the test. As badly as I wanted to hop off the chair and play with him, I knew I couldn't as my father was in the chair right next to me on the left. I pretended not to see the boy, and he drew closer, now sitting backward in the chair right in front of mine so he could face me and get my attention. And even if my father hadn't come to this particular appointment, I knew not to play with colored kids or Dr. Schultz would tell my father.

I thought, *This is such an easy test to pass if only this boy would stop asking me to play.* He was being so funny as he tried getting me to look his way as if not falling for my shy act. Sitting there with a straight face was hard since he made it extremely difficult not to laugh. I didn't know what else to do, so I looked to my father, hoping he wouldn't yell at the boy and call him bad names but instead would guide me out of the boy's direction. My father pretended he knew nothing of what was happening even though I knew it was an act of not seeing since he's deaf, not blind.

Leaning over to whisper in my ear, my father said, "Tell him no, you are dirty and black."

I did not want to say that to the boy; he seemed nice and didn't deserve to get spoken to like that. Since my father was hard of hearing, I changed the words up. "No, you are dirty, you need a bath."

I loved when my mother said that to me; I loved taking baths, but even saying what I did, I upset the boy so much that he teared up and ran over to his parents. I could see how proud my father was of me, and it made me so angry at him that I let my brain tell him off as I spoke in silence, calling my father a deaf bastard, an asshole dick, and more. Afterward, my mother and sister returned to the waiting room, and we were leaving when the boy told his parents something. They gave my mother a look of death. As she put it once, she learned what had just happened in the waiting room she left me in, trusting I would behave. Now outside of the doctor's office and walking to our car, she shared how the mother and father of the crying black boy were giving her a look of death; she didn't know why and assumed they must be racist, but why was she getting such a look as the boy was crying? And then my father told her why as he cracked up laughing at my behavior. Growing irritated with my father for being so racist that he found it humorous how I acted disrespectfully, my parents began arguing.

My mother told my father, "You know, Adolfi, if you weren't so fucking racist, she wouldn't learn that shit."

My father cut her off right as she mentioned how he's only racist because of his father, and he told her, "No, you're always telling her that she's filthy and turning black and needs a bath. It's your fault she said that to the poor little n———."

That night, I felt guilty for being happy to have passed the test and would be getting a puppy while my mother cried in her room as my father made her have sex forcefully for speaking ill of his father. I was glad I now shared a room with my sister and not my parents anymore, but the pain of knowing my mother was hurting and hearing her begging for him to stop was just as bad.

Since I chose the puppy, my mother said my sister gets to name her. Ada chose a perfect name for our new puppy, Greyhound. My father wasn't pleased with her naming my puppy, but I told him I wanted the name Ada chose because I loved it; this way, he would agree to name the puppy what Ada chose. Mommy was right when she said it was only fair Ada gets to name our puppy.

After picking up our newest edition to the Averbach family, my father teased my sister the whole ride home and said, "You might have got to name her, but that's Ilse's puppy."

When my mother tried telling him that was not right, he laughed it off, saying it was just a joke and bitched her out for not being able to take a fucking joke. I didn't understand what his problem was. I didn't think of Greyhound as my puppy. She was the family pet. We would all be allowed pet her, play with her, and teach her new tricks. I thought, *Maybe this puppy can help me teach daddy how to be good. That will be one of the tricks I teach her.*

My father wanted to show her how to play with the hose water as Sweety does whenever Joe turns on his hose. He turned the hose on and pointed the streaming water toward Greyhound, but she took off running, scared; it was the cutest thing I ever saw. My father also thought it was cute until trying again and she reacted the same way as she did the first time. He went downstairs to the basement and came back outside with a hammer and a stake. He banged the stake until it was secured to the ground and used a small metal chain he had lying around in the basement that he could attach to the stake. After connecting the chain to Greyhound's collar, he turned on the hose and squirted her. Greyhound tried her hardest to escape, but she couldn't break free. Growing irritated and yelling at the puppy he claimed was mine, my father then began making the hose water splash in Greyhound's face, and she was yelping and trying even harder to break free.

My mother had been pleading with him to leave her alone because he was scaring her, and now Mommy was yelling, thinking he "is" deaf, so maybe he wasn't hearing her. My father became furious with her, "How dare you talk to me like that outside. What do you want the neighbors to hear? This dog is stupid. She's nothing like Sweety. What the fuck did we get her for?"

My sister and I were trying hard not to cry when my father unchained our puppy, picked her up by the back of her neck as her mother would, and began beating her on her backside. As he walked toward the back door to go inside, he opened the door, flinging Greyhound into the kitchen, and then went to pick up the mess he made in the yard.

My father angrily said, "Girls, go inside and do not baby that mutt! Rosewitha, do something useful with your life and help me clean up this mess."

Everyone obeyed, afraid of what might happen if we didn't. Knowing it would take at least a few minutes to clean up, my sister and I gave Greyhound love and apologized for what our father did when he's angry for no reason. Once we heard the sounds of our father closing the basement doors, we made our puppy hide on him and ran to our room to play.

CHAPTER 12

"Not Mommy's Michael!"

One day while my father was at work, Imani and I asked our mothers if I could play in her yard, and we were so happy when they said yes. My mother chased me as I ran excitedly to the front, and I heard my mother call out, "Ilse Leigh, do not leave that gate until I get to you, and I'll walk you over."

Imani and her mother met us in their front yard, and while our mothers chatted a bit more, we ran to the backyard to play. Imani's mother followed us after my mother went back inside and told me that my mother said for me to call her when I was ready to come home. I loved Imani's mother so much, and I felt so bad especially knowing that she knew how my father was. I had so much respect for her as I tried to have for my mother because even knowing this, she still accepted me as her daughter's best friend.

A short while later, out in Imani's front yard, her brother's friend came over riding his bike and asked for Pokey. Imani's mother asked her to run inside and get him, and Imani threw her head back while screaming, "Pokey!"

Her mother said the same thing my mother had said to me and my sister, "I could've done that myself." I was dying of laughter at how funny Imani was being.

Pokey came outside to greet his friend and said he needed to go to the backyard, and as his friend was still sitting on his bike, he hurried off, threw the bike on the ground, and yelled, "Pokey, wait up!"

Imani and I were cracking up as she pointed and said, "Look at his big butt." His butt had been big to where it protruded outward as he ran off to catch up to Pokey.

After we finally calmed ourselves down from the uncontrollable laughter, Imani told her mom she had to go to the bathroom, and she ran inside. Her mother then asked if I had to use the bathroom, too, since neither Imani nor I had used it in a while, and I responded, "Yes, please." She was amazed at my manners and couldn't help but laugh as we went inside. Imani came out of the bathroom, so it was my turn, and her mother showed me the way. It was the same way as my living room was to my bathroom at home. I went in and closed the door behind me. I lifted the lid and was surprised to see brown poop in a house of a brown family. I flushed the toilet, not minding that Imani was probably so excited that I was over and she forgot to flush her poo when she finished. I wasn't sure why, but I thought that since I am white and poop brown, brown people must poop white.

After I finished and went back to play, I asked Imani, "Why is your poop brown?"

Looking confused, she asked, "What color is your poop?"

I said, "Brown, but I'm white. You don't poop white?"

Now wanting to know the answer to my question, she said, "Let's ask my mommy."

We ran to her mother, and Imani asked her our serious question. She burst out laughing and immediately called my mother to tell her, and right away, you could hear my mother laughing hysterically through the phone. While they spoke about how kids say the cutest things, Imani and I went to play with her dolls. She had colored dolls, and I begged her to let me hold the baby doll. I wasn't allowed to have any colored dolls at home. As Imani and I played, I felt very proud of myself to have learned that not only do we all bleed red but also we all poop brown or sometimes blue or green.

Another day, while my father was home from work, my mother had been listening to her Michael Jackson record. Since my father didn't have hearing aids in his ears, I was dancing and singing along. Once he got in the shower, I paid close attention to when he'd get out, and when my father did, I immediately stopped dancing and went to play with Greyhound and White Tiperella so my father would think that when I was dancing before he got in the shower, something else was playing and that once mommy changed it to Michael Jackson, I stopped listening and did something to distract myself from hearing it as would any obedient German daughter.

My father put his hearing aids in and asked my mother if she could take the girls out to a relative's house for the day or something so he could rest peacefully, claiming to be feeling under the weather. My mother never passed up an opportunity to get away from my father for a while, especially when she knew he wouldn't be bothering her, calling the family looking for her to say "Get your ass home now."

After we got ready, my mother brought us to our grandma's house, which didn't last very long as she could only take so much of OJ's behavior, so we left and went to my aunt Faith's house. I loved going over there even though Sasha was always a bitch to me, but I loved her anyway. And also Noah and Daniel, but Jennifer and her parents were who I loved hanging out and bonding with. Whenever Jennifer wasn't home, I'd hang out with the adults and make them laugh at my silliness. I loved my aunt Faith and uncle Jakob so much, and they loved me the same.

I liked to pretend I was going to grab my uncle's ginger ale bottle, knowing that he'd widen his eyes and raise his bushy white eyebrows and say, "Oh, no, Lee Lee, this isn't soda. It's an adult drink." He never realized that I never drank ginger ale because I didn't care for the taste; I only did it to play around with him and bond. I didn't care that my father told me I was not supposed to respect anyone in this household; I did the opposite of what he said.

When we got to the house, I saw Jennifer wasn't home, but Aunt Faith said she would be home soon and had gone to a friend's house. I tried hanging out with my sister and Sasha, but I could only handle so much of their attitudes and calling me names for no reason, so I hung out with the adults in the kitchen until Jennifer got home. She wanted to listen to music so I could hear all the "cool" new songs that just came out on the radio. My cousin knew I liked her taste in music.

After hearing a lot of "awesome" songs I knew my father would never approve of, Jennifer had to use the bathroom and asked me to stay on her bed until she got back. I didn't listen. I saw a pretty bottle of some pink stuff and decided to make myself pretty, putting it on my eyelids like eyeshadow. Everyone heard me screaming, and once they all got to me, my mother noticed a bottle of nail polish opened on the floor. I dropped it onto the floor once my eyes began to burn, and I couldn't open my eyes to see where it went to pick it up. While my mother was fighting with me to wash my eyes, she and my aunt explained that nail polish does not go on your eyes, only your nails.

Jennifer was still upset that I could've gotten hurt even worse than I did, and she blamed herself for leaving me alone even though it was only a quick bathroom run. The nail polish bottle was sitting on Jennifer's dresser, which led to her conclusion that I had climbed the dresser to get the nail polish. My cousin told me that when she was younger, she also climbed her dresser, and it wound up tipping over, falling on top of her, causing her to get hurt, with some of her fingers breaking. Jennifer and I had such an emotional bond after that, and I promised not to climb on her dresser anymore or touch her nail polish. Jennifer let me pick a color from her nail polish. I chose another shade of pink, and then my big cousin painted my nails.

It was getting dark out, so my mother decided we had better head home. Once we arrived home, we saw that the outside light wasn't on. My mother hated that my father never cared to turn the light on for her as she had to juggle two tired girls in a dark house since he never bothered to turn on those lights either; it was a waste of his electric bill. She'd always shake as she tried to get the key into the door handle, afraid of the serial killers who roam the streets in the dark that my father repeatedly warned us about. I wasn't scared of serial killers because my father always said that serial killers don't go after people who stay home and read some good books. My mother and my sister always read books, and they always read books to me. We had a lot of good books. I was worried about the raccoon who attacked Sandra and chopped off her tail, wondering what it would do to us. It would probably eat us alive.

Once we got into the front foyer, my mother turned on the light, and she noticed something was all over the floor in the living room but couldn't quite tell what it was since the living room had minimal lighting that gleamed in from the front foyer light. As we got closer and she turned on the lamp in the living room, we saw broken pieces of records scattered through the room and into the small hallway that led to my parents' room, my sister's and my room, and the bathroom. As my mother walked through our tiny home, she found Greyhound who was in a corner chewing on a record, and she screamed, "Not my Michael!" She was crying because it took a lot for her husband to finally agree to let her have a record of MJ under his roof. She knew he wouldn't agree to it a second time.

As my mother cleaned up all the broken pieces, she sighed in relief when she discovered Greyhound had only chewed up her records and none of my father's, afraid of what he'd do to Greyhound if she did. Her tears turned into anger at the fact that the only reason she left the puppy all afternoon into the evening was that he said he was sick. She started cursing him out to herself, saying we would have stayed home if she knew he was going to "suddenly feel better" and take off to God knows where doing God knows what.

Once my father returned home and learned what Greyhound had done, he praised her for it and gave her so much love while he told my mother it served her right for even listening to that n——, slut, and faggot music. My father kept teasing my mother as I sat there, wishing I could scream at him to stop. He told her he hates that she lets me listen to it, and he does not want me to listen to it.

My mother brought us to our room, put us to bed, and gave us good night kisses. Not long after, I heard my father tell my mother, "Take off your underwear." So I hid my head under my pillow and cried myself to sleep.

CHAPTER 13

Dollar Bill Needs a Home

In a rage, my father confronted me about visiting the black girl in the welfare house next door, teasing that the color of the people's skin was brown as the color of the house was brown also. I told him no. Technically, I wasn't lying since it had been a few weeks since, and he was questioning me about the previous week only. He complained that if I couldn't abide by his rules, I would have to get disciplined, and he hadn't even corrected me yet for listening to the n—— music, stressing that he caught me and I couldn't even try to lie about that since he saw it with his own eyes. He reminded me again that my life was like the princess in *The Princess Bride*, and he had my every move watched. My father told me if he heard it again, he would have to quit his job so he could be home, raising me to be a "true" German, instead of my slut mother raising me to be a slave like her and her family.

I did not want my father to quit his job, so I knew I would have to be more careful when I played with Imani; maybe we could only play over the fences in our backyards like usual. I knew it couldn't have been Joe and Jessica across the street or Rosa and Adolfi next door because everyone but Rosa was never home during the day. Rosa knew about our secret friendship but also knew my father could not know about it. I was thinking of who could have told when suddenly my father punched me in the right side of my chest for daydreaming again when he needed me to concentrate. I hated having to "concentrate" because my dear old dad always started from the beginning of life to the present day, and I must obey my father and our fathers before him. I was born "with a choice" to be like Adam or be forced to be like Eve. I didn't understand why he always had to bore me with his true beliefs when I knew my beliefs didn't have to be proven to be true since they were real. Once he caught me wandering off daydreaming a second time, he told me how stupid I was, demanding I go to my room and play with my toys like a baby, so I did, and we went to World War 3. My army kicked the Germans' racist asses.

The next day, my mother, hesitant to tell me that White Tiperella was nowhere to be found, came to me, and I knew she was trying to find a way to say that our kitty was lost. It was already midday, and I knew after I woke up that she was missing. I ran past the couch, and White Tiperella didn't come to chase me and attack my legs, so I walked back to look underneath, and the kitty wasn't there. I asked my mom for my baby kitty, and she told me she was outside. I also kept hearing my mother take her bag of food and shake it as loud as she could, hoping our kitty would come running, but she didn't on any of the countless times my mother tried. Then my mother called my grandma and told her the cat's been missing since last night.

I didn't know the cat was missing since the night before, and now I was worried and felt guilty because I had so much fun playing that I fell asleep early. I felt like maybe if I tried calling her since I knew how to do Daddy's call with a very high-pitched "Here, kitty, kitty, kitty, kitty," which always got her attention when my mother's food trick didn't work. She would be home playing with me, clawing and biting me, and making the pain of my father's life lesson go away. But I heard in my mommy's voice that she's been holding back tears all day, so I did not want her to see me upset; that would make her more upset. But there we were on the couch, her telling me that our cat was missing and us holding each other while our tears rolled down our faces. Then it happened "all over" again once she picked up my sister from school and we had to tell her the news, and now all three of us were crying hysterically.

When my father got home from work, he didn't seem to care about the sad news; he just said she was a slut and was probably out whoring the streets. He was more concerned about where his dinner plate was, saying, "Buddha, Buddha needs fooda, fooda." He found it to be no excuse for my mother not serving him on time since it was just a fucking cat.

Since my grandfather didn't rent or own a home, he had to depend on his children to take him in. Neither Aunt Anna nor Uncle Jakob was willing to take him in; they weren't so forgiving for everything he put them through growing up. So Grandpa lived with Uncle Heinrich. My grandfather did not believe in the homeowner being in charge; he felt he was the elder, so he laid down the rules of the house. Refusing to allow this to continue, Uncle Heinrich kicked his father out of the house, leaving him homeless in just his Lincoln Town Car.

Grandpa drove straight to his son Adolfi's house to cry about how he was old and homeless since Heinrich kicked him out, so my father didn't hesitate to offer him a roof over his head, hoping he would win his father over his brother and finally be his favorite son. My father came into the house to tell my mother that his dad was moving in, and even though she wanted to say no, she unwillingly agreed to let him stay. My mother was unaware that her husband was not giving her a choice. It was torture having Grandpa live with us because not only was he meaner than my father, but also he would do the most irritating things for no reason. He did stuff that one could barely tolerate with just a visit, and now I had to live with it, causing my parents to argue, and then that night, my father would make my mother have sex, and I could hear Grandpa laughing on the couch in the living room.

When being called by my mother, Grandpa would pretend not to have heard her until she used his preferred name, Dollar Bill, which at first she had to figure out on her own by realizing, "He is a money-hungry bastard. Let me turn his name into dollar signs, and that will get his attention." And so it did. Grandpa also loved letting me know how much he loved his grandson, Heinrich, and that he gave him all kinds of money and presents, and then he'd hand me a single dollar bill. And he always pretended to fall asleep on the couch, and when my sister or I would walk past, he'd put his foot out and trip us. Not only did we fall and hit the floor, sometimes, we got hurt, but our father would yell at us for disturbing our dear old grandpa while the elder was resting, saying we never know when Grandpa won't be around anymore.

I would go to my secret happy place and dream about what it would be like when he was no longer in my way as I was trying to save my father. I loved my grandfather, knowing he was this way because of my great-grandpa, but I also hated him for making my father think that a father is not supposed to love and protect their children and wife and that he's allowed to rape his wife and beat his children. I imagined my father was a puppet and my grandfather was his master. My father's face changed, as if under a spell, whenever he would try to train me for World War 3. It wasn't his usual happy or angry face, the only two emotions I'd ever seen him express. And now, with Grandpa living with us, my father was even worse. Having to go down to the basement to learn about tools, ropes, tapes, and slaves with just my father was enough trauma. Now I had to do it with both him and my grandfather. If my father was at work, I had to go down there alone with the man I had to call Grandpa. I learned what it's like to have my mouth and nose covered with rags or tape. Grandpa would tie my arms and legs together. He would cut me with his pocket knife and then warn me I had to lie to my parents and say I got it from playing too close to the sticker bush out back. My mother would say to be more careful while my father would yell at me for it.

A form of training he could do out in the open was what he called a game with a song. While bouncing the ball in the right beat to the words of insults, I had to learn the lyrics, "Bouncy, bouncy bally, my sister's name is Paulie, giver her a smack, break her back, bouncy, bouncy bally." He had also taught my sister the game, and Aunt Anna knew the game. I knew I wasn't allowed to tell them what the "real" game was: a song from a chosen sibling to their slave sister, and they must get their slave sibling to sing along and play something secretly about them. I would think of my version while trying to sing his version, "My grandpa's name is Paulie."

One day, while my sister was at school, my grandfather made me practice in the backyard. Imani had been playing outside in her backyard, and her brother and his friend were with her but in another part of their backyard. When I noticed Grandpa wasn't paying attention, I'd peek over there. It wasn't that she was trying to get my attention as Imani knew we had to pretend we didn't talk. I just wanted to be allowed to play with her instead of having to obey my grandfather, who was wrong about everything he said and did. Then he told me to go to the gate and put my fingers together as you would when calling a dog and say, "Here, n——, n——, n——."

I knew it was wrong to do that, but I also knew that Imani knew I wasn't racist, and I thought that if I did it to my funniest face, she'd know it was just a joke. I asked my grandfather if I could play with her after, and he grunted and said, "Yeah, sure." I ran over the gate so excited to have gotten permission to play with my friend and did what he said, exactly how I wanted to look while saying it, especially since my back was facing Grandpa.

As soon as I did it, Imani ran to the house crying as I called for her to say we could play. I saw her brother and his friend go inside the house after her. It was hard not to show that I was upset, but I knew I hurt my best friend's feelings, and now I also knew that even turning it into a joke was hurtful. I did to her what my family did to me, and I was so angry at myself for it and furious with my grandfather for making me do that. He was proud that I had accomplished his goal, but now he knew there was a strong chance I had been sneaking a friendship with the black neighbor.

My mother got a phone call from Imani's mom and immediately called me and my grandfather into the house. I obeyed her; he didn't. She told me that she got a call from Imani's mom who informed her of what I did and that they both knew I did not just decide to do that myself and my grandfather made me do it. As my mother went on the porch to confront my grandfather, he tried denying it. My mother stated that someone had seen my grandfather leaning over me, showing me the calling-a-dog motion with his fingers before I walked over to the fence, doing it myself.

Right away, my grandfather began cursing my mother out, disrespecting her in her home, and when she pointed out that this was her home, her rules, my grandfather angrily said, "Eh, fuck you, bitch. This is my son's home." And he went to the front yard to sit in his car and wait for his son to return home.

When my father arrived, it didn't take long before he came storming into the house, demanding an answer as to why his elderly father was kicked out of the house and into his car, especially when the weather was getting chilly outside, swearing he could catch pneumonia easily. My mother told him what happened and that she did not kick him out; he left of his own free will. My father busted out laughing over what I had done. Then they got into an argument, my mother saying that was not how she wanted her children raised, and my father stressed that was how he wanted to raise his daughter. It wasn't until my father could no longer put up with his father, thinking he could tell him what to do in his own home, that my grandfather made up with his son, Heinrich, and moved back in with him.

While you could not say our house became more peaceful, it became more tolerable, only having one abusive grown man living in the house. But even then, my friendship with Imani had ended since it would not work out, being I was the daughter of a racist Nazi.

CHAPTER 14

Christmas Traditions

Most people who celebrate Christmas wake up early, excited to open presents. My mother had a different tradition which I wasn't too fond of the year prior, but this time, I didn't mind because I knew I would wake up to open the beautifully wrapped presents lying underneath the tree. My mother's tradition was that Santa came at midnight, and once he finished placing our gifts under the tree and in our stockings, he would leave, and our mother would come to wake us. Then after we opened all our presents, my sister and I had to bring our new stuff into our rooms, with the help from our mother, and then we played in our room while she cleaned up.

While she was busy getting the house back to where her husband would approve of its tidiness, our father came into our room to be sure we weren't playing with too many toys at once, and he would annoy us while we tried to play in peace. When my mother was all finished, she came in and played with us for a short while until she couldn't stay awake much longer, and she helped us clean up our toys and tucked us into our bed with just as much love as if she hadn't already tucked us in just a few hours ago.

My father had his tradition where we watched Christmas classics, and I had to listen to him tell his version of how the movie was supposed to be understood. My mother and sister were lucky as they were sitting a short distance away on the couch, but I had to sit on his lap while he told me which actors and actresses I could meet and must obey and which people were slaves. Oh, how he loved all the villains in the movies, and when they had gone soft, he'd tell me that was not how the story goes. If it were a new Christmas movie, we were forbidden to watch it until he had seen it first. Another tradition was a story he'd tell his children about how there once used to be a real Santa, but his name was Old St. Nick; he did deliver toys to children as the story goes, but one year as it was snowing and the rooftops were icy, Old St. Nick slipped off the roof, breaking his neck as he landed and immediately died.

Holidays were not a special occasion when my father would relieve his family of his abusive ways. Christmas was as great as my mother tried her hardest to make it while my father criticized everything she did or said. I chose not to go along with him picking on her and my sister, so I got picked on too. Even as far back as Halloween, he didn't want me to celebrate, but I did anyway. Thanksgiving, I was supposed to watch *March of the Wooden Soldiers*, but it was extremely boring, and I just wanted to see my shows that had holiday episodes airing, so I went into my parents' room with my mother and sister. I liked that television better than the one in the living room because it was yellow and had dial buttons to work the TV.

So once the Christmas music began playing on the radio, my father started to get people to join in and tease me about my four front teeth again. I loved Christmas music, but that song was torture for me. I couldn't wait for the radio stations to stop playing Christmas songs. He would have my sister sing it along with him, and sometimes, he'd yell at her after because he needed to release stress on both of us. And this year, when we were unwrapping our gifts (since my father was an occasional smoker and was on a cigar kick), he had put his cigar down in my mother's antique ashtray and walked away to use the bathroom. I noticed it was still burning and ran over to put it out for him so it wouldn't start a fire. Once I got to it and picked it up, the lit part started hurting me, so I quickly broke it in half. I did not realize that I didn't know how to put cigars out correctly, and I got a bad feeling in my gut once I heard my father coming back. My mother didn't even see what had happened because she was distracted by my sister needing her help.

When my father walked over, I sadly told him about my mistake, and as I thought he was just going to bitch me out about it, he grabbed me by my tiny wrist, lifted me in the air, and repeatedly flogged my rear. My mother, screaming at him to put me down, now learned that he made the careless mistake of leaving a lit cigar down for someone to get burned. As he complained that I wasted his money, my mother defended that one of her children could have gotten hurt and that he had no right to beat me for his mistake. She demanded that he no longer puts his hands on her girls. I wished my mother would stop yelling at him. I didn't want to have to hear him make her have sex, but that's why I knew I had to convince Mommy to tuck us in longer this time so that maybe I would fall asleep before she left our room, or Daddy would fall asleep before she goes into their room. He fell asleep because once Mommy went to her room, I didn't hear anything but Daddy's snoring and Mommy trying to roll him over so she could fit in the bed, and then I fell fast asleep.

CHAPTER 15
A Child's Report of Abuse Will Be Unfounded

At the beginning of 1987, we had to take another dreadful trip to my great-aunt Bertha's house. My father needed me to be on my best behavior and obey the orders given to me while we were there, unlike how I usually try to get away with not obeying my superiors, like being told to disrespect a slave and I respected them instead. He was tired of me being respectful to the slaves and disrespectful to my superiors, especially the elders. So before it was time to get ready to go, while I was watching *Bambi*, my father sat down with me to talk about the German rules and all that Nazi garbage. Getting irritated that I just wanted to keep watching the movie, my father told me that if I didn't start obeying, my mother could wind up just like Bambi's mother, leaving me no choice but to abide by the rules since she would no longer be around to teach me how to be a dirty, slutty slave.

When the part where Bambi's mother got shot in the beautiful meadow came on, I imagined it being my mother, and even though I wanted to cry, I knew I'd better not, or I'd get "something to cry about." When we went to the Satan-loving community, I felt so sick to my stomach as I thought, *If I disobey, who will try to shoot my mommy in a meadow? Probably my grandfather since he hates her so much. It couldn't be my un-great-aunt Bertha since she has arthritis in both hands. She probably can't hold a gun or shoot it.*

I had to distract myself and stop thinking such bad and scary thoughts, and instead, I thought of something that made me feel better. I thought of how my aunt was in constant pain with her arthritis and how I wished her hands would fall off. I thought how bad it would hurt if I squeezed them as hard as I could. I hoped her arthritis was deadly and wished that when we got to the house, my uncle Hans and aunt Maple would say, "I'm sorry, Adolfi, your aunt has passed away. Her arthritis killed her."

As reality settled in and we pulled up to the house, I felt shaky knowing how I had to act to keep my mother alive. During the visit, I was to treat my mother like a slave. So when taking off my coat and shoes, I threw them toward her and refused to pick them up so she had to pick them up. When I said hello to everyone, I did not slip and call Hans or Maple my respective names for them, Uncle and Aunt. I acted like a pain in the ass but showed much love and appreciation during the brief moments I could to make up for it. Then since it was sunny and not too cold out, my sister and I were told we could go outside in the backyard to play.

We were running around on the grass, with my sister running in front of me with her golden hair flying in the wind. We were having so much fun until my father and his aunt called me over to them. I ran to them, hoping they'd be quick so I could get back to playing with my sister. I learned that Bertha did not like how my mother dressed me in something that matched my sister's outfit as a mother would dress her twins. My father told me I was to run up to my sister and call her a blonde dick. I had to do the stupid hand movement that he did when he'd call her that: pointer finger out, wave your hand in a circular motion as you say the word blonde, and then as you say the word dick, you point your finger at the person you are saying it to.

While I did not want to hurt my sister's feelings, I did as they said, and when I pointed in my sister's face, she smacked me. I wished she hadn't done that because I knew she would have to go to the discipline room. Bertha told me to hit her back, but I had had enough of her stupid German rules, and I told her no. She looked at my father and said her favorite line, "Adolfi, you know what you must do." We both had to go into the discipline room and got beat with a belt, one child at a time. As the belt banged against me repeatedly, I thought about how beautiful my sister looked in her yellow dress with black polka dots and how ugly I looked in mine.

At my sister's school, they had been teaching the students about abuse, encouraging them to report it if they suffer abuse at home. My sister, tired of being abused and forced to watch me get beatings, decided it was best to tell the teacher that Daddy beat her and her sister with a belt. I was home with my parents and had to disrespect my mother all day as per my father, so my mother decided to leave me with my father while she went to visit family until it was time to pick up Ada. The phone rang, and by my father's reaction, I knew it was not a good call.

"Hello? She did what? Oh, I'll fix her ass, thanks for telling me."

I thought for "sure" someone was telling on me for being a good person, and I was going to get one of the worst beatings of my life. My father came into my room, sat me on my bed, then sat beside me and said, "Your sister did a very stupid thing. She told someone that I beat you girls with a belt, and now CPS is coming here."

He explained that he doesn't abuse us; it's discipline. Then he warned me that if I told them he beat us with a belt, they would take my sister and me away from our parents, and we'd get separated, and then I'd never see my family again. He said that once you get put in the system, you get abused far worse, possibly even killed. He claimed to be lucky to have people in the school district watch us; otherwise, he wouldn't have gotten notified, and we wouldn't know what to say to convince CPS not to take us. And once he was sure I was all prepped and ready, he mentioned that he would have to prepare Ada as soon as she got home. Then when my sister and mother arrived, my father prepped them both.

As CPS showed up, I was terrified of losing my family. I wouldn't be able to watch over my mother and sister to make sure they don't get killed, and I would never be able to change my father's evil ways so that he can go to heaven when he dies. I would never see my puppy, Greyhound, again. I could not allow that to happen, so I put on my happiest face to show CPS that I was not a victim of abuse. My mother, unaware that my sister and I ever got beat with a belt, decided that since her firstborn lied about abuse, I might do the same. I had been jumping on my bed a few days prior, and since she couldn't stand near me at that time, she asked me to stop jumping before I fell and could get hurt, and she noticed I was getting closer to the edge where my dresser stood next to the bed. It had been a day that I had to disrespect her, so I didn't listen, plus I was having fun and didn't want it to end. It did end when I fell, and my temple hit the corner of the dresser, then I fell to the ground. I didn't mind so much; I liked the pain, and now I would have a bruise to push on when I needed to feel pain.

Being I had a bruise at the corner of my right eye, my mother told CPS what had happened and added, "So if Ilse says one of us beat her, that's another lie."

She couldn't understand why Ada had made such a false accusation. I couldn't understand why my mother could think that I would lie when she taught her children that lying was wrong. And even though my mother didn't know it, my sister was not lying. When the CPS workers questioned us alone, my sister apologized for making it up, and we convinced them that we were well-raised children who were not victims of abuse at home. They said they would make one more pop-up visit but let my parents know the case would be unfounded.

The next time I tried to watch my favorite movie, I could not watch *Bambi* without crying my eyes out, so my mother wouldn't let me watch it when I asked to, knowing it would break my heart when Bambi's mommy got shot. When my sister or I were hurting, so was our mother as our pain became her pain. She'd convince me to watch one of my other favorites, *Cinderella* or *Sleeping Beauty*. I saw the villain as one of my father's superiors and I was the princess, but in my imagination, I wasn't the only princess; my sister was a princess too. When Maleficent changed into the dragon, I imagined it being my grandfather. Great-Aunt Bertha was the wicked stepmother of Cinderella.

CHAPTER 16

A Chosen One with a Choice to Make

　　Even though CPS was no longer involved, my father's aunt no longer trusted to allow my mother and sister in her home. She told him they were no longer welcome and I had a choice to make, obey and follow my father's path or become a slave like my mother and sister. If I chose my mother and sister, I also would be banned from returning to the community. So my father broke the news about my mother and sister getting banned from his aunt's home, hoping I would agree to obey all the German rules. Once he verbally laid out my choices, I chose to love everyone. When my father sarcastically asked me if I wanted to be a slave, I said no, so he decided we had to make a few trips to a few places, thinking maybe I would have a better understanding of having a choice without having a choice.

　　The first place we went was the Satan-loving community where my father showed me all the beautiful houses and property, telling me that someday I could also have a beautiful home of my own or even more than one, adding that I could have as many homes as I wanted if I would obey. When we drove closer to the house we knew well, he asked, "Which house is your favorite?"

　　I pointed to the one I knew I was supposed to if I didn't want Daddy to get angry. He told me a short version of his story growing up. My father had to treat his mother and sister like a slave and respect his superiors like his father, grandfather, and aunt, Bertha. I was so relieved that the story didn't take as long as usual but still annoyed that my father couldn't see the correct way of life. He was showing love and respect to the wrong people and hurting the ones he loved and who loved him back.

Our next stop was my aunt Anna's house. I was so happy to see her, and the first thing I did was give her the biggest hug and kiss as I heard my father's joy from my love for his sister whom he secretly loved. The next thing I did was play with my favorite toy, my aunt's half-red, half-yellow charm necklace that had all kinds of silly charms attached—a boat, a toilet, a stop sign, and more—and I'd pretend the animal charms or the people charms were using the toilet bowl. I'd make the sounds of someone peeing or pooping and make everyone who saw laugh until tears fell from their eyes. I played with that necklace every time I visited my aunt. She would sit there and take each charm off to make it easier for me to play, and she'd play with me and make the sound effects too. And every time she took them off or put them back on, she'd show me how she did it so I could learn how to do it myself.

On this particular visit, my father had been in a rush and was annoyed when she took them off and suggested I play with them still attached to the necklace. My aunt brushed it off and did it for me anyway. When he said it was time to get ready to leave, my aunt and I began putting the charms back on the necklace. My father was growing more impatient, having to make one more stop in time because he had shit to do later, too, and he couldn't have me with him. After scolding my father for being such a grouch when she was bonding with her niece, my aunt smiled at me while informing me that I could keep it, stating, "It's a gift from Aunt Anna's heart." I felt so warm, loved, and special to have a gift from my aunt's heart.

The last stop was my grandmother Daisy's grave. I was so happy to have visited her after seeing her daughter whom I knew my grandma wanted me to love. As my father and I stared at my grandmother's grave, he told me her sad story again as he made it clear that he didn't want me to end up in a grave too. He spoke about how other slaves weren't so lucky to have a grave as some get disposed of like the garbage they were. He warned me that he didn't know what the future had in store for me if I chose to be a slave.

I looked at my father and said, "Daddy, I miss Grandma Daisy."

He chuckled and said, "Kit, you never met her. How can you miss her?"

I replied, "I love her."

He couldn't help but show his appreciation hearing me say those three words about the mother he missed dearly but could never reveal his secret to anyone but me.

It was windy out, but I was unsure if that was why I saw a single tear fall from my father's eye, and once he saw that I was crying, he did not say I was going to get something to cry about. Instead, he leaned down and hugged me, and I kissed my fingers and smeared them across her name on her gravestone. My father scolded me because the grave was full of filthy germs, and we left.

On the ride home, knowing he couldn't bring it up inside, he asked what my choice was, so again, I said, "I love everyone, Daddy."

He wasn't angry about it. My father understood, especially after going through an emotional day himself. He didn't have to tell me for me to know that he felt such pain visiting his mother's grave, wishing she was still alive and could have met her granddaughters. He shared that he knew our grandma would have loved us. Then he tried to get me to change my mind by telling me I could no longer be a patient of Dr. Schultz and that I would have to go to the health clinic where all the welfare recipients go.

That night, as I lay in the bed I shared with my sister, I was still upset. Now as the house was quiet, I started thinking about everything from before I was born to the present day and how none of this was fair or even allowed to be, and I just started crying, trying so hard not to be loud.

My sister heard me and asked, "Ilse, why are you crying?"

I knew I couldn't tell her, so I replied, "I'm not."

She got frustrated with me and said, "I can hear you. Stop crying for no reason. I have school tomorrow, and you're keeping me up."

Even though it wasn't her fault that I couldn't tell her, I got mad at her because if she only knew, she would not have said I was crying for no reason. I decided to tell her part of the reason and said, "I miss Grandma."

She told me Grandma was well and that she was home asleep, which was what we should be doing.

I said, "No, Grandma Daisy."

She sighed and said, "Ilse, you never even met her. Now please stop crying so I can get to sleep."

At that point, I was too angry to cry. I couldn't believe what I heard her say. I wondered if she was just being cranky because she was tired or if she did not miss our grandma even though we never got to meet her. I started to play in my mind that I "did get to" meet my grandma, it was my grandfather who died, and that my father never turned evil. It was such a relaxing and soothing time to feel like my grandmother was alive and well, and I fell fast asleep before I could come up with a plot on how my grandfather died.

CHAPTER 17

Training for Deadly Situations

Although my father understood my wanting to love my mother and sister, he did not appreciate it. He told me that while I was under his roof, which I would be until age twenty-one, I still had to obey him, and now he had to train me to get out of deadly situations that I most likely would face when I moved out on my own. He said that for the time being, he could keep a close eye on me to make sure no one tried to kill me, but once I no longer lived under his roof, he would no longer be able to. He told me he was hard on my sister and me because he loved us and didn't want us to die. He then told me how disappointed I had made him, stating that my sister was a natural-born slave, needing training from the beginning, but I was born with a choice, and he could not understand why I chose slavery.

I did not understand why he couldn't realize that I did not choose to be a slave as I chose to love everyone. My father tried, as he had before, countless times to bribe me with jewelry and riches that I could have if I changed my mind and then let me know I could change my mind twenty years later, and he would still accept me and so would God. I just told my father I was not changing my mind, and then he threw me down on my bed, one hand around my ankle, pinning it down to the mattress so that I could not break free, and the other hand to tickle the bottom of my foot. My father had always tickled me and sometimes even my sister, but he only held her down to torture-tickle her foot like that, never mine until now. At that moment, I realized why my sister hated daddy's tickle time; it didn't tickle very much as it was painful torture.

Not having changed my mind, on the nights when I used to go with my mother and sister for family bingo night, I had to stay home with my father because he needed my mother gone so he could practice drowning me in the bathtub. I hated when my father gave me baths as it was because he always made the water way too hot. When I would ask him to add some cold water, he would tell me, "No, it'll cool off, and your body will get used to it. Just sit down and stop acting like a baby." Then he'd bitch, knowing my mother must be wasting water just to please me, which, in turn, cost him money, and he always let the water pour into my face and eyes. He never covered my eyes like Mommy always did.

Now, he would tell me to lay on my back in the water, and once I did, he would submerge my head underwater and ask who I loved more, him or my slut mother. He would say, "This is what happens to dirty sluts when they don't obey."

I had to practice holding my breath for as long as possible because I didn't know how long he would keep my head underwater. I could feel my breath running out; my body would tremble, and when he'd finally let me up, I'd be coughing and gasping for air, trying so hard to catch my breath. I wasn't allowed to play with bath toys either. I had to get out of the water straight away. It wasn't until I was in my room that I could play with my toys like a stupid baby. I couldn't wait for my mother to return home; I missed attending family bingo night.

It was a night that my grandmother and a few of her daughters would meet up at Starlight Bingo Hall and try to win some money; my favorite thing to do was slip under the table with my younger cousins, trying to find other money that was dropped on the floor by others or their bingo chips. I loved when I'd see the stampers. It felt like hitting the jackpot. And I would show my little cousins all the different colors of gum that people had stuck under the table, and I let them know not to touch the chewed gum because it was nasty germs and they could get sick.

My mother would constantly keep gently pushing on me with her foot to make sure I didn't wander off too far, and when she couldn't feel me, she'd look under the table and say, "Ilse Leigh, get off the filthy floor. C'mon, this is why I don't like bringing you because you don't know how to listen."

I did know how to listen, but I didn't feel the need to sit at the table along with older people as they were screaming "Bingo!" My cousins wanted to play under the table, and so did I; I didn't see the problem. Plus, sometimes, I liked being yelled at by my mommy because I knew she wouldn't hurt me like Daddy always did. I loved when she'd get so fed up with me that she would say, "That's it, I've had enough." She would smack me on my arm, hand, or sometimes my bottom, but it never hurt; it tickled, and I would laugh and say, "That tickled, Mommy." She'd reply with, "Oh yea? See if it tickles next time. Keep it up with me, Ilse Leigh." But next time, it tickled just as it always did.

In another part of training, my father would punch me in my chest on the right side. He'd ask if it hurt, and when I'd say no, he hit harder than the last time. He told me he wouldn't punch me on my left side because that was where my heart was, and he didn't want to kill me. That was the whole reason for training so that when someone tried to kill me, I won't die. He'd tell me how much he loved me and loved my sister, too, and he did not want us to die, especially me, because I looked just like him, adding that I was his favorite. My father always said that he felt something special about me.

One day, while my mother was home, I had been sitting in my father's La-Z-Boy chair, and he came over, telling me to get up in a playful voice, so I looked at him and playfully said, "No, Daddy."

Since I had the footrest out, even though I didn't come close to reaching it, my father lifted his leg and stomped down on the footrest to close it, sending me flying out of the chair, and I face-planted on the floor by our couch. My mother saw this, screamed at my father, and ran to pick me up. She grew even more protective of me after seeing blood gushing out of my nostrils. I couldn't help but cry since it was so painful.

My father told my mother, "Oh, I was just kidding around with her. It's not my fault she can't take a fucking joke."

As he went to tell me to stop crying or I'd get something to cry for, my mother interrupted him by screaming, "She's fucking bleeding, Adolfi. You could have broken her nose! She went flying in the air like a fucking ball, that is no fucking joke."

He would not show remorse, and I didn't get to sit with my father in his chair right after while he babied me as usual when he hurt me. Eventually, he asked me to come over to sit with my fat daddy so he could talk to me. He told me he didn't want to hurt me, but I needed to learn what I would go through once I turned twenty-one, and if I didn't toughen up now, I'd never survive. Then he laughed at how funny it looked when I flew off his chair and admitted he thought I would hold on; he didn't know I would fly off and get hurt. Now that I would have another bruise to push on and the pain stopped being so unbearable, I laughed with him and admitted that it was fun until I landed and got hurt.

He smiled and said, "I'm sorry about that, kitten."

*****

My father made a family trip to Mystic Bay Park, and while walking the trails, he made sure that he and I were distanced from my mother and sister enough to where they wouldn't hear him. He softly explained how people dragged slaves through these trails and find spots to bury them where their bodies would rot away. He hated when people would drive through the trails for walking and that it would interrupt him from teaching me "very important" life lessons. He'd say how dangerous it was because they could run us over, and now I was distracted by the tracks the tires left behind, straightening it out so you couldn't see the tire tracks anymore. It wasn't as if a car drove through while we walked the trail, so I wasn't afraid of getting run over. I wasn't concentrating the way he needed me to be.

Annoyed, he asked, "Do you want to get killed and then buried here and I will never find your body?" I shook my head, and he said, "Then pay attention."

He allowed us to walk with my mother and sister, and he began talking about all the serial killers that come out at night and kill children and sluts. My mother hated when he'd talk like that and asked him not to, but he ignored her and continued telling his story about serial killers. When she asked again for him to change the subject, he yelled at my mother, saying she needed to stop trying to shield us from the dangers in the world because if we got killed, it'd be her fault.

Later, when we left the park and my father had me alone in another room of the house, he told me that since I am a slave, I have to let men do what they want to me or they will kill me and bury me at the park or beach somewhere, and there's nothing else he can do about it. When my mother got my sister and me away from our father, she apologized to us for our father being so paranoid and thinking we were going to die, and she assured us that we would not die.

My sister and I were well aware of my father's paranoia as he usually had to have the doors to the house locked and the blinds and curtains closed. He always said how someone might try to walk right in and kill us all or he'd accuse a possible burglar of wanting to come and steal his stuff. He was never concerned about our belongings.

My mother would say, "We don't have any stuff that someone would want to steal," and "We live in a shit shack."

I wondered why my father kept us enclosed most of the time, but sometimes, he would break his rules and let a little light shine in the home.

With the short time spent training me, my father needed my mother to be out of the house more, and he needed it to be somewhere where I couldn't tag along. He noticed that I was sneaking and telling my mommy I did want to go to bingo with her, and she would take me when he needed me home.

He began making fun of her for not having graduated school to the point she thought about going back to get her GED. It wasn't long until my mother started night school twice a week. It didn't matter that my sister was home. If he didn't want a chance for her to eavesdrop on our conversation or lesson, training would take place in our basement. He'd leave my sister upstairs alone with no one watching her, not caring if she would get hurt or need help with something. She was not allowed to interrupt us no matter what. It wasn't an order he worried about her not obeying since she and my mother knew that they were not allowed in the basement unless he was down there and said they could.

When he wasn't going to be home, he'd lock the doors so no one could get in. Sometimes, he'd need time alone with my sister, but he would never leave me alone, so he would have my sister closed in the bedroom with him while I had to sit in his chair in the living room and watch TV with the sound loud so that I could not hear. Sometimes with the TV as loud as it was, I could still hear my sister screaming and crying, and he'd yell at her, "Stop crying or I'll give you something to cry for." She'd obey and not make a sound, or I could not hear her.

It didn't matter if my father had put on my favorite show or movie; I was too worried about my sister to want to watch. I wished I could run into the room and make him stop beating her. I once went to sit on the couch before he went into the bedroom with her so I could hear, but he yelled at me to stop trying to eavesdrop, mind my own business, and demanded I get on his chair. I thought back to the day he flung me out of it and thought, *Oh, now I can sit in your chair, you stupid deaf bastard.*

Since I was powerless and couldn't find a way to stop this, I just sat on the chair, pinching my legs as hard as I could so I'd feel the pain. I thought it was unfair to my sister that she was getting beat and I wasn't. But sometimes, we had to get disciplined together, and I had to start doing what my sister had been doing for as long as I remember; we had to stand in separate corners of the living room, facing the wall with our arms out straight, palms facing upward. My father would hand one of us the yellow pages, and the other would get the white pages. He would announce that Ada had twenty minutes and I had ten, and if we lowered our arms, he would give us a beating, and then the clock would start over again.

CHAPTER 18

Cheers to Beers

My father suggested to my mother that we start inviting her family over for barbeques since the weather was getting nicer. Knowing there were many alcoholics in the family, my father said he'd be sure there were plenty of beers and food and we'd all have a good time. I loved the idea of the family coming over for dinner. Usually, my father never invited people to eat over. There were times when since most of my mother's siblings didn't live too far from each other, someone would pop up unannounced, and we had been sitting down eating our dinner. My father made them wait in the living room until we finished our meal. I could see the sad look on my little cousins' faces. I hated that he did that; we always had leftovers unless it was leftovers we were eating. Whenever we'd go to family's houses when they were eating, they always offered some; if there weren't enough to give, they'd offer something else.

Once my father suggested having barbeques, I was excited to have family eat at my house. It felt like a dream come true. My father informed me I was old enough to drink now, but no one could know, not even Mommy. He said he would be filling up his special Budweiser glass with beer for us to share, but I had to wait until all the adults were acting silly enough and were distracted. I knew kids weren't supposed to drink, but I liked that my father wanted a special bond with me; he loved that Budweiser glass, and so did I. I loved how the cup was clear and I could see the beer was sudsy, looking like a bubble bath in apple juice or something.

I was finally going to be allowed to drink out of it, so when he told me to hop up on fat daddy's lap, I excitedly hopped up as my father playfully grunted, pretending that I crushed his legs. Everyone said how cute I was, my father's twin. And as soon as no one was paying attention, he told me to start drinking. He didn't warn me about the taste, and I figured that since root beer and cream soda were sudsy, that beer would taste like soda, but I was wrong; it was the nastiest drink I had ever tasted.

It made me gag, so I looked at my father and said "I don't like it, Daddy" as my face clenched uncontrollably in disgust.

He got angry with me for wasting time and said, "You wanted to be a slave. I let you make that choice, but since that's what you chose, you don't have a choice. Now drink up."

Knowing what would happen if I didn't obey, I listened to my father and took sips every time he said drink. Everyone seemed to be having too much fun to notice. They never even smelled alcohol on my breath. As for my mother, I wasn't allowed to get too close to her; if she tried, I had to do something to piss her off so she'd walk away. By the time everyone left and it was time for bed, I already had a bunch of snacks, plus I drank soda and brushed my teeth, so the smell was gone. But to be on the safe side, I had to pretend I was already falling asleep so she'd kiss me and walk away. I wasn't allowed to say good night or that I loved her. I had to hold my breath until she moved away. But she'd always say it to me anyway. It hurt a little, but my sister said it to her if she was still awake, and I always said it in my head.

Down the strip of Warlock Rd., the cross street to Darkened Circle, was a bar named Smitty's Pub. It had a picture of a naked woman sitting in a wine glass outside above the door where the name of the bar was. My mother hated that and hated how everything was about sex, even in cartoons for children. She had mentioned it a few times, and my aunts would agree. I wondered what it looked like inside there whenever we would go pick up my father and relatives who went with him. Sometimes, it would only be Noah and Daniel, and sometimes, Willy went, but most times, my father invited Uncle Jakob Miller, knowing he could not turn down a bar run. My father said he had to keep him nice and drunk so he would stay out of the way of him training his boys. And now since my father thought I chose slavery, I had to see what it looked like inside.

The workers were so kind to me. After going the second time, I sat at the bar and slammed my hand on the counter, saying, "I want my usual."

Even customers were laughing, and the lady behind the counter said, "One soda coming up."

I knew it wasn't just soda because I felt warm and silly inside my body, but I was glad it wasn't beer. It still tasted gross but not nearly as bad as beer. At least the soda made it go down easy. I didn't gag once like I constantly did with beer.

As my family was hoping that not bringing me to Great-Aunt Bertha's for a bit, plus the alcohol they were feeding me, would erase my memory, they had to put me to the test. My father drove me there and told me to point when I saw our aunt's house. He was surprised when I did and told me how smart I was and how proud I made him, and right after, he reminded me that I could only go there again if I obeyed all the German rules. When he asked me to be on their side, I looked him in his eyes and said, "No, Daddy, I want to love everyone." His face became angry as he scolded me for being so fucking stupid that I couldn't even follow simple rules and how I'd rather be a slave than be rich and successful.

My father did not understand that I didn't need to be evil just to become successful. If Daddy only knew my plans and the army I had started building since I met Bowie at his hot dog truck, he'd be so proud of me. He would never call me stupid again. My father would have appreciated things and people, and he would forever be thankful to me that I saved him and everyone else I could.

I then wondered why it had been nice out for so many days but we had not gone to see Bowie. Now was my chance to start telling him everything my ancestors did and everything my family and many other bad people were doing in the present time as well as their plans for the future. I practiced speaking for so long, and I needed to see Bowie so together we could start building our army.

Once my father was in a good mood and wanted to bond with me, I held his face and looked him in the eyes, "Daddy, it's nice out, can we go see Bowie soon?"

He smiled wide in amazement that I remembered Bowie while he said how smart I was, and he corrected me, "Kit, it's Barry, not Bowie."

Then my father told me that the blacks started taking over the reservation, so he got the hell out of there and we couldn't go to see Barry anymore. The words repeated in my mind over and over. I lost my chance to save the world with Bowie by my side. I didn't care what my father said. I remembered that Barry was his real name, but he liked when I called him Bowie, and anytime my father tried to correct me, Bowie would tell my father that I could call him Bowie if I wanted to.

When I reminded my father of Bowie saying I could call him that, he angrily replied, "Yeah, yeah, yeah, you can remember that, but you can't remember how to obey." Then he called me stupid and told me to get out of his face.

After more family gatherings with plenty of beers and more trips to Smitty's Pub, my father drove me to the community where my great-aunt lived. I hated that he would not give up and understand that I liked that I was "banned" from this place and I never wanted to step on the grounds of evil Satan lovers again. It annoyed me that my father kept asking me to follow the devil instead of God.

I told him I was banned, and he replied, "Yeah, just pay attention. They built a house just like your great-aunt's house, and we can move into it, but it's your house once you are old enough to own it. All you have to do is choose us. Your mother and sister can come, but you must treat them like the slaves they are. You don't understand that you are special. You're not like them, you are a chosen one."

He then pulled over to a house that looked much like my great-aunt's house, if not exactly like it. I couldn't tell if the houses were close to each other. I didn't even know if it was on the same block. While I was very familiar with this place, it was becoming a little unfamiliar.

My father looked at me and asked, "What ya say, kitten?"

I looked him in his eyes and said, "Daddy, I can be successful and buy a house like this, and I can love everyone."

His face grew angry, and he started telling me how stupid I was, that I'd never be able to own a house like this or at all, and that slaves are not successful. And since that was what I chose, to be a filthy slave, I will never be able to own anything since I'll have to be on welfare. I didn't mind people being on welfare since my aunt Faith and her family were on it, and they got food stamps. Sasha loved taking my sister and me to Warlock Rd. with our mothers. We'd get snacks and drinks; we had so much fun. Sasha always got along with me on our walks to Warlock Rd. or when my mother and aunt would go for walks, picking up bottles and cans to make a little money so they could afford to go to family bingo night.

I got lost in thought, remembering all the family walks as every single one was like an amazing adventure for me. My father caught me daydreaming and scolded me even more. As soon as we got home, I had to stand in the corner of the living room with the yellow pages for ten minutes, and then I had to play with my dolls like a baby. I didn't care. At least he didn't beat me, plus holding up the phone book wasn't so hard anymore as I was tired of getting beaten for lowering my arms and having to rewind the clock, so I stopped allowing my arms to lower. It hurt my arms, back, and legs, but I did not care. It burned, but nothing like when I burned myself with the coffee or when Daddy always burned me in the tub. I told myself I could do it, and I did.

CHAPTER 19

Children Are Not Seen or Heard

Usually, when we'd go to my grandma's house, I'd always hear Aunt Greta say children should be seen and not heard. Then all the kids had to go upstairs to Anja and OJ's room. I didn't understand why she said that because by doing that, the adults couldn't see or hear the children unless they made a lot of banging sounds. When Aunt Greta said those words, I never had to listen, but now she yelled at me and told me to stop pretending that I was too scared to walk up the stairs and to stop acting like a baby, accusing me of being jealous of the new babies that had recently been born in our family.

It seemed like someone in the family was always pregnant, sometimes more than one family member at a time. When my mother tried to tell her that I could stay downstairs if I wanted to, Aunt Greta snapped at her, saying all the kids have to go upstairs because she wanted to talk freely and claimed she couldn't do that with me being nosy and listening in on their conversations. I never even cared what the adults talked about; they always spoke freely, whether children were around or not. She convinced my mother that I should be seen and not heard.

I was so angry because I did not like her children. I certainly did not want to play with them when no other cousins were around to defend me. My aunt Alana had come over with little Jakob earlier, but they always got him to join their side just like they always did with my sister. I didn't understand why they needed to have sides at all. It reminded me of my father who always wanted me to join his side. But this was even more annoying because they didn't want anyone to be on my side.

My mother, afraid I might fall going up the stairs, walked me up them, and I asked, "Mommy, can we just go home instead?"

She said she didn't even finish her first cup of coffee, and then she'd have one more cup and we could go home. I told her the kids were always mean to me, so she said, "You call me if they misbehave, and I'll come up and make them stop. If they keep it up, you can come back downstairs."

I excitedly replied, "Okay, Mommy."

Then she reminded me that she did not want me walking down the stairs by myself, so I had to call her if I had to go to the bathroom or anything.

When we got upstairs, Anja had all her expensive Barbies out with their beautiful gowns and outfits and accessories. Usually, she would always say I had to play with the cheap dolls our aunts and uncles bought for her. Anja and OJ enjoyed making fun of the relatives who refused to buy them expensive stuff. Meanwhile, they did nothing to deserve a gift at all. They also had a habit of rubbing it in my sister's and my face that our grandma always bought them expensive toys but all the other kids in the family got cheap toys, claiming she didn't love us as much as them. What Anja and OJ didn't know was she hated having to buy them expensive shit; she'd rather give them coal, but her daughter and her son-in-law would not allow her to give them cheap gifts. It had been something all her other children tried telling her, that she did not have to do what they said, especially being they lived in her house as they didn't even contribute much to the household. But my grandmother would say how it's always like a zoo in the damn house with the kids doing anything they wanted and their parents not giving a shit what they did.

Then there was Otto who was always watching his racist shows with the TV on blast when he would be in the living room. And her daughter, Greta, always picked a fight with her younger-minded sister, Heidi, so my grandmother tried to keep the peace as much as possible. But this time, Anja invited me to play with the dolls she had out for her and my sister to play with. OJ and Little Jakob were playing with his wrestling action figures, and everyone was getting along. My mother told all of them to be nice to me or they would have to hear her mouth once she heard about it, and they all smiled and said how welcome I was, so my mother went back downstairs. They filled me in on their storyline, and we began to play. I was so happy my cousins were finally being nice to me.

Some dolls were children while others were adults. OJ took his action figure as Anja took her Barbie over to him, and they made their dolls kiss. It was weird, but I figured adults kiss other adults all the time, so that didn't bother me. It was when they made their dolls hump one another that I had to say something. I knew kids should not play sex stuff. I've seen some of our other cousins get in trouble for doing that and more at their houses, and even before they'd get in trouble, I'd tell them that was not how to play as I'd show them the correct way. OJ snapped at me and said he didn't give a fuck, and if I wanted to play, I had to play their way. I let him know that my mother said they have to be nice to me, and OJ laughed, saying, "I don't give a fuck what your mother says. She's not my mother."

Angry that he spoke that way of my mother, I looked at my sister who told me to play how they were playing. I told OJ, "Fine, I'll tell your parents."

He replied, "My father says I can do whatever the fuck I want, so go ahead and tell."

I said, "Fine, I'll tell Grandma."

He started teasing my grandmother, saying she was not allowed to tell him what to do, that she's not the boss of the house. I had heard enough, and I angrily replied, "She is the boss of the house, and this is her fucking house."

Then I walked to the door by the stairs, opened it, and yelled, "Mommy!"

Anja and OJ told me that if I dared say anything, they would tell my father I cursed and I'd get a beating. When my mother opened the bottom door, seeing me at the top of the stairs, she asked, "What's the matter, baby?" I told her I had to go potty.

As she walked up to get me, I looked over at my cousins, who were pretending to slice their throats and an impression of me getting beat by my father. I looked at my sister, and she looked lost in thought, a sad look on her face that told me she was not on their side. I could tell at that moment that she did not like how they played with the toys and she did not want to, so they were probably making her too. Little Jakob had the same kind of face as my sister. Once my mother walked me to the bathroom, it took me a bit to go, thinking if I should tell my mom or wait and talk to my sister later. I figured that was probably better because if my sister told my mom with me, Anja and OJ wouldn't tell on my sister for something bad she did because they hated that my father gave her beatings. They only loved when I got beaten by my father. I would have to ask my sister not to tell Anja and OJ that I told on them too.

My mother then began getting irritable as she held me up so I wouldn't fall in the filthy, shit-stained toilet and said, "C'mon, Ilse, do you have to pee or are you just playing? My arms and back are aching."

I told her I did, and then I finally started peeing. She said, "It's not your fault that no one cleans this damn bathroom for your grandmother. They are such filthy fucking animals, I swear."

I told my mom I agreed with her. She laughed and said not to repeat that, so I told her, "I won't, Mommy. Can we go home now?"

She replied, "Not yet. I just finished my first cup and would like one more."

I knew that meant at least another hour, so I asked if I could stay downstairs and play, but she told me no because she was enjoying the peace for a bit and also didn't want to hear Greta telling me what to do anymore when she doesn't even correct her own damn kids. So once my mother helped me wash my hands, she walked me back upstairs where my sister and cousins were playing with their pillow pals and making a tent with blankets from Anja's bed to OJ's. I was glad that they put the dolls away; I could not play like that, and I was not going to allow them to make me.

My sister may have let them tell her what to do, but they were not my boss. I had hoped that maybe they'd forget all about it and we could play like kids were supposed to. I liked what they were playing this time until they knew for sure that my mother had gone downstairs and wouldn't be coming back up. That's when it got very uncomfortable again, and this time, they told me that I had to do sex things with them. I told them no, and OJ punched me hard in my arm, telling me if I thought that hurt, I should wait to see what it feels like when my father beats me. Anja told my sister to kiss me and rub my chest and vagina, only she called it a pussy like the adults do. I hated that word and what they were trying to make us do.

Luckily, my sister said, "No way, I am not touching my sister. I'll do anything else you tell me to but that."

OJ said, "Fine, I'll do it."

He walked over to me, kissing me and touching me. I smacked his hand away, so he punched me in the same spot he had before then continued what he was doing before I tried to stop him as Anja and my Ada were doing sex stuff with each other. I told myself that everything would be fine once we left because I would talk to my sister and we would get our mommy to stop this shit. Then it switched, and I had to do sex stuff with Anja while my sister and OJ had to do sex stuff together. OJ then told Little Jakob to do sex stuff to me, but as he started, my aunt Alana called him and said to come downstairs, telling him it was time to go home.

I knew that was a good sign because my mother should be finishing her coffee soon and then we could get the hell out of there. While Little Jakob was getting his shoes on, my mother came to the bottom of the stairs and yelled, "Yeah, girls, come on! Start getting ready. We're going home now too."

It was like music to my ears as if the heavens had been calling me from above. My mother yelled again, "Get your shoes on. Let's go, Ada Rose, Ilse Leigh. And, Ada, you make sure you walk your sister down so she doesn't fall. I gotta take my last sip of coffee and wash my cup so Grandma doesn't have to do it later."

We were already getting our shoes on, and neither she nor I could hide our eagerness to leave. I knew my mother wasn't actually telling us about how she washed her cup before leaving; she was saying it as a hint to her sister, Greta. Greta wouldn't even lift a finger to wash a dish as she never cared to clean their shit stains off the toilet.

Back at home, where my father was waiting for us to get home, growing angrier each minute that passed, he immediately started yelling at me once we walked in. He claimed that I left my room a fucking mess, with my clean pajamas thrown on the floor and toys not put away. He demanded that my mother and sister stay in the living room while he made me clean it up. As I thought I knew I did not leave the room a mess, I knew the consequences if I had. We entered the room, and I clearly saw I was correct, only I didn't fold my clothes how he expected them to be. But I did place them under my pillow as I would have to wear them again for at least two more nights. The toys that were left out were the toys I would be sleeping with, placed neatly in front of my pillow as my mother let me do. Mine weren't as neat as my sister's side because I slept with more toys than she did as I needed to sleep surrounded by my army for protection. I also did not know how to lay them as decoration, so he made me fix them while he told me that I was not obeying, saying that I chose to be a slave, so when one of my superiors told me to do something, I must abide.

Singing the same old song, he preached about Adam and Eve, how Adam was her superior, how she bit that forbidden fruit when not only did Adam tell her not to bite, but also did God. And for that, women were forever sluts for all our time here on Earth. He told me how people at NASA were working on going to space to be able to create life up there, like in the cartoon *The Jetsons*, because God would be destroying the earth and all the slaves would die with it, except the ones who obey because people will still need slaves. He told me whenever I was ready to choose his side, I would be welcome with open arms and he'd never turn me away. He reminded me that I was special because I was born a chosen one, so I don't have to be a slut if I don't want to, but I have to start obeying and must choose the "true" path.

Then the subject changed to the presidents from the past who have ruled the US, the present one, and who will be president in the future. I was tired of hearing all these names my father kept saying;

I didn't care about them or their plans. They would make God have no choice but to destroy Earth so they could live in space. I could not understand why none of them could see how silly that sounded. I could hear my father say something about how sex sells and all slaves must obey or die, and he asked if I wanted to die. My response was the same as usual, "I want to love everyone. Sorry, Daddy." I smiled as cutely as possible and said, "I love, my fat daddy!"

He was frustrated with me but couldn't resist my cuteness as he tickled my armpits and belly. I was having a great time now after having the worst day of my life. But the tickles became torturous once my father moved to my feet; he held one leg down with his hand around my ankle while he pinned it to the mattress and tickled the bottom of my foot very harshly. When he let me go, I thought I was free until he grabbed my other leg and repeated the steps of what he did to the other. Then finally, he set me free for real, and he left my room.

My father asked if I wanted to watch my favorite movie with him, *Cat's Eye*. I was so excited. I loved that movie because Drew Barrymore was in it, but even more because that kitty was so cute. This time though, my father stressed how Drew Barrymore was a good girl since she obeyed James Woods and all her other superiors, telling me she was also born a chosen one. I didn't understand how that could be since her hair looked blonde to me. And he made me keep my eyes open on the scary parts like the room where they put the smoker's wife to electrocute her and the cat.

When they put the woman inside, my father asked if I wanted her to be my mother, and I said no. He said, "Then start obeying your superiors."

This time as I watched. I couldn't look away from the gremlin monster when, in the past, I was allowed to close my eyes. Just the way he moved was scaring the hell out of me; forget about the sounds he made. Once the movie ended, I went to my room since I didn't want to bond with my father anymore for the moment. My sister, already in there, questioned what I was looking for as I looked frantically at the bottom of every wall in our room.

I told her, "I'm making sure that ugly gremlin doesn't try to come to steal our breath. We don't have a cat to save us."

At first, my sister started cracking up. "Ilse, it's just a movie. That thing isn't even real."

I asked, "How do you know?"

She said she just did. That was not a good-enough answer for me, so I continued looking for holes forming in the walls. As I thought to myself that I would not give this monster a chance to break a hole in the wall. My sister snapped at me and called me stupid, yelling at me to cut it out.

She was really pissing me off, so I snapped back, "No, you're stupid and ugly." I then did the whole hand motion as I called her a blonde dick.

She yelled for our mother and got me in trouble for cursing. She didn't realize she'd be getting yelled at as well until I told my mother why I called her that. After her initial angry reaction, my mother sat between us on our beds and talked about how siblings should stick up for each other, not put each other down. She said how she hated that our father picked favorites and he constantly made us tease one another and that it was very wrong. Then she spoke solely to me, assuring me that no mini monster would be breaking holes in the walls to steal my breath, that monsters weren't real and they were for entertainment. She told me if I was too scared to watch them, I didn't have to anymore.

She didn't know that I didn't have a choice, so I just smiled and said, "Okay, Mommy."

After she kissed us good night and tucked us in, I was finally going to be able to talk to my sister about what happened to us. When I called out "Sissy," she responded with attitude.

"What? I'm mad at you for getting me in trouble. You already get to be Daddy's favorite. I should be Mommy's favorite, but you keep trying to take her away from me because you want to have everyone and leave me with no one."

I tried telling her that she got herself in trouble and it was just getting us into another argument, so I told her to have a bad night's sleep, and I pretended to be going to sleep, and we left each other alone for the night.

She just responded, "You have a bad night too."

I had to say it because I wanted to scream at her, and when one of us did that, Daddy comes in, and we get a beating.

On the next visit to Grandma's house, OJ made us watch porn he borrowed from his father. I hated porn since my great-aunt and my grandfather used to make me watch it at her house. I chose not to go there anymore, so I was not going to watch it at Grandma's house, and I said I had to pee and went to call my mom. OJ said he'd walk me down, promising he would not let me fall. I said okay and trusted him to take me. Thinking he would walk me down and go right back up, he waited downstairs for me. My mother grew irritated with me as I couldn't go, and her arms were sore from holding me. I could hear my grandmother yelling at OJ for picking on Uncle Henry, and then she yelled, "Oh, go back upstairs, will you, ya little shit?"

He replied, "I'm waiting for Ilse. She can't walk back up by herself."

I asked my mother if I could play with Uncle Henry, claiming I thought I had to pee but I didn't. She was glad to get me off the toilet and said, "Yea, he could use some cheering up since your cousin doesn't know how to respect him and treats him like shit."

Walking out of the bathroom, I tried to ignore that OJ was there and went straight to my uncle sitting in his chair. As we played, OJ began bugging me to come back upstairs. Still ignoring him, I got off my uncle's lap and tickled his belly. He put his fingers in the pinching position and said, "I'm gonna pinch your hiney."

I loved when he did that, and I playfully moved from side to side as he tried to pinch my hiney. He then stood up, and I knew he was going to chase me, so I started to run when OJ grabbed my arm and made me run with him to our grandmother's room, screaming, "Henry's a rapist, run!"

I could hear my mother's anger as she jumped out of the kitchen chair and stormed into the room, screaming, "What the fuck did you just say about my brother? He's not a rapist, and that is your uncle. You start respecting him."

My mother never laid a hand on other people's kids, barely even her own, as her spankings tickled, but I thought my mother would give him the beating of his life. Usually, when someone in the family screams like that, my heart raced, and I would be scared, wishing I could run and hide. This time, I was hoping she'd do it. I was tired of OJ's shit too. I wished he and his sister were not my cousins. They didn't love me or my sister, and though they're nicer to her, they treated us both like garbage just as they did the family they did not respect. OJ went back upstairs, and shortly after, his father came downstairs, taking over the TV with his racist shows. He yelled at me for bouncing around and told me I had to sit and watch with him. I didn't want to watch his stupid shows; he watched *Bonanza* and *Little House on the Prairie* and other shows with bad actors who enslaved good actors or other innocent people. These famous people were evil, just like my father's side of the family. They hated people of color and women and children.

I told him no since I was playing with Aunt Heidi and Uncle Henry, and he yelled at me for disrespecting him and telling him no. Hearing all this, and the fact that she just had to say something to OJ about disrespectfulness to an uncle, my mother scolded me too, and then Aunt Greta put in her two cents, "This is why I say 'children should be seen and not heard,' so, Rosewitha, take her back upstairs, please."

My mother did and spoke to me about respecting my elders on the way up. I was hoping my mother would catch them watching porn, and I was going to let her know that Ada didn't want to watch it, OJ made her, but instead, OJ was taking out his video game stuff for Nintendo. After telling OJ he better behave with me, he apologized to his aunt Rosewitha, trying to be cute like I did to butter my mommy up. "Sorry, Aunt Rosewitha, I'll be good."

She said, "Don't apologize to me. You need to apologize to your uncle."

He said okay and told me to come and play video games. OJ never allowed me to play his games, but he handed me a remote, so my mother went back downstairs. Once he heard the bottom door close, he turned the game off and put the porn back on; I didn't have a choice now but to stay up there and do what he said. I hated my life so much; I just wanted to die already.

CHAPTER 20

Dear God

I had had enough of all the racism and kids doing sex stuff. I could not handle how crazy people thought they could take over the world, so I decided I would start praying to God. I would pray to the real God, not my father's true God. I didn't know how to pray since my father was always showing me his way as he'd also show me how to properly hail the dead guy, Adolf Hitler. I recalled seeing kids pray in movies and shows, and they kneeled on the side of their bed with praying hands and would say "Dear God" as they continued their prayer. So that was exactly what I did, hoping my sister had fallen asleep already.

I learned she was still awake when she opened her eyes and asked what I was doing, suggesting I was looking for holes in the walls again. She didn't know that I had already done that before she came into the room for the night, and I told her I was praying to God. She told me to go to bed, claiming I was keeping her up even though I was talking in my mind only. When I told her I was not making noise since I was talking in my head, my sister told me I was making noise and she could hear me moving around.

My mother heard us bickering and came to find out what the problem was. Ada told her I was playing around when she was trying to sleep, and I told her that I wasn't playing; I was praying to God like the kids on the TV do. She told my sister to let me pray and then told me to hurry up, pray, and go to bed. Our mother kissed us good night again, and we said I love you, and she left as my sister let me be, and I began my prayers.

I tried not to ask too much and asked God to please help me find Bowie so we could form an army and stop all the evil Germans who wanted to take over the world. I told him I knew violence was not the answer, but if that was what it came down to, I was sorry but that's how it would have to be. I promised him I would send all the evil people back to their countries, but if they do not leave, my army and I will have no choice but to send them back to where they came from, being unborn. I figured I'd throw in an extra prayer and ask, "Oh, and, God, can you please get me a beautiful pair of red bang shoes like Dorothy's ruby red slippers in *The Wizard of Oz*? I'd like that, thank you, and I love you. Amen." Then I went to bed, falling asleep as I thought Dorothy was not a slut as my father told me she was; I wished I could grow up to look just like her.

The next day, as I played with my toys, preparing a World War 3, something happened that I couldn't explain. I felt like I was "frozen in time" as someone was trying to send me a message. First, I could feel something in my heart, and then I felt it in my brain. I could not see or hear anything around me. However, I received the message sent to me. My brain told me it was from God, that he did not want more violence, he only wanted peace. He stated that no one has a right to decide when someone's life will end, only he decides when it is their time, and although it is painful, it's the natural way of life as we all must share our time here on Earth. Then once we pass on, our souls join the heavens for all eternity. However, the ones who sin in the worst ways and do not wish for forgiveness will have to join Lucifer in eternal hell because he does not want misery in heaven. He said even people who do very evil things may have his forgiveness as he will always love all his children. He said he knows who is genuinely sorry for their sins and who is not. God told me this was how he wanted me to introduce myself to whoever I feel will want to hear, "Hi, I'm Ilse Averbach. Yes, I have a German last name, but I am nothing like my ancestors who sinned in the past or the ones who sin today. I do not believe in enslaving people—no one is a slave. And no one has the right to decide when it is someone's time to die. Only God says when it is their time."

My brain finished relaying the message, and I could now see that I was in my room. I noticed I had still been sitting in the position I was in when I got frozen still, sitting on my feet while leaning over with the hero toy in one hand and the bad one in the other, giving each other a chance to surrender or fight. I was a little worried that God was watching me, so I threw them into the toy box and looked around to see if I could tell if he was.

To make sure, I asked, "Can I have the red bang shoes?"

My brain was silent, and I didn't freeze in place, so I knew my answer. I told my brain to tell God I was sorry but I still hated the evil people who won't change for good. And if it's war they want, then war is what they'll get. They could simply go back to Germany, Italy, or wherever they came from, but they don't want to. I waited for God to have me frozen again, but he didn't. Then I ran to my mommy so she could wake my feet up from their sleep.

The next time we went to my grandma's, Anja and OJ showed my sister and me a shark game. I was scared of sharks because I always had to watch *Jaws*, so I told them no and went to play with Aunt Heidi and Uncle Henry. They went behind the curtain of the bay window in my grandmother's living room and started saying some stuff. I didn't know what they were saying, but my sister had come out from behind the curtain. Anja and OJ were still behind the curtain and repeated what they said before. Then they moved the curtain with such force as it swayed to the side, and my grandmother yelled, "Stop that shit before you rip down my curtain."

My sister ran to my grandmother's room as Anja and OJ chased after her, pretending to be sharks. It did look fun, so after the second time they did it, once they came back into the living room, I asked if I could play too. I told them I didn't want to be in front of the curtain; I wanted to be a shark. They told me no because I didn't know the words or how to play the game, so I had to be a person running from the sharks. I told them I was too scared, and they laughed at me. My sister didn't laugh at me since she knew why I was so afraid of sharks, so she came out from behind the curtain and said she'd be a person with me. I loved my sister so much for that. The game was just as fun as it looked. My heart was racing, and I was nervous and scared when our cousins chased us, but I loved every minute of this new shark game. I couldn't wait to learn the words so they would let me be a shark for a change.

Just as I started thinking that, my wish was coming true; the fun I was having turned into embarrassment and shamefulness. I ran into my grandmother's room and jumped on her bed. I was about to jump off and run back to the living room, but OJ jumped on the bed and tried kissing and touching me like he did the last time we were over. I knew I would have to pray even harder tonight; this was not supposed to happen. Kids weren't supposed to do sex stuff, especially blood-related ones. Whenever my other cousins got caught doing sex stuff with each other, my aunt Betty's husband, Wilheim, and my aunt Greta would say it was normal and that it's called kissing cousins. My mother would say, "Fuck no, it's not, it's disgusting. Kids should not be sexual with each other, especially not blood-related ones."

Trying to think of a way out of the mess I was stuck in, I jumped off the bed, informing everyone that I wanted to be a shark this time. While they did follow my lead and left the room, they still wouldn't let me be a shark, so I told them in front of my grandmother, "I'm not playing anymore 'cause you won't take turns being sharks."

Grandma heard me and yelled, "Share with Lee Lee. I'll rip the damn curtains down. I don't give a shit anymore!"

Then my mother, who came into the house after finishing her cigarette, added, "Ada Rose, Ilse Leigh, get away from your grandmother's curtains right now!"

And that was how I knew my plan had worked, game over. It didn't take long before Anja and OJ did what they wanted anyway and continued. I was already sitting on the couch with Aunt Heidi to my left and Uncle Henry to my right, sitting on his chair.

As my mother told my sister not to play with the curtains, Aunt Greta said, "It's okay, they are all getting along. They were only fighting because Ilse didn't want to follow the game rules. I saw the whole thing."

When my mother brought us home that night, my father was furious with me. He demanded my sister stay out of our room until he said so and that I follow him. First, we went to the bathroom where he showed me the crumbled-up toilet paper I had left in the garbage pail before we left. I didn't understand the issue since that was where we always threw the toilet paper. He told me I was lazy and too stupid to know how to neatly roll the toilet paper around my four fingers and then wipe and throw it away.

He added, "Instead, you always gotta be so sloppy and just crumble it up. Now let's go in your room."

He grabbed me by my arm and forcefully walked me toward the room, my tiny legs barely able to keep up with his speed. He pushed me in and closed the door behind us. He started talking about Adam and Eve again. What that had to do with toilet paper, I did not know. Next, he warned me that if I didn't start obeying my superiors, he would have to quit his job and raise me the right way and not how to be a slut like my mother showed me. He was really pissing me off, calling my mother a slut when he was the one and the only man she slept with. She never went anywhere without at least one of her children at the hip; she was going to school, but it didn't last long until my father made her quit. When she'd go out to play bingo, Ada always went, and sometimes I could, but I usually had to stay home and get disciplined for something and didn't know what I even did since my father never made sense to me. I had been teasing my sister whenever he told me to and disrespected my mother when he told me to. Not that I wanted to. Daddy would say if I didn't do what I had to, my sister would get beat or would say someone I love would die.

Finally, when he was preaching and teaching me about survival, he said something I liked to hear, we were going to the park that weekend. Of course, it was only to teach me a lesson about what would happen if I didn't start obeying, but I didn't care since I'd get to visit my angels.

That night when I prayed to God, I told my angels I would see them at their grave site soon. I slept peacefully, knowing they were excited that I'd be stopping by to pay my respects.

CHAPTER 21

Obey Orders or Get Thrown into the Waters

That weekend, we went to William's Wildlife Park and Refuge. I was upset because I wanted to go to Mystic Bay Park; it's bigger, and there's more for kids to do, but this park had my angels too. We went to the boardwalk, and my father managed to get me away from my mother and sister to where they couldn't hear, just like he always did. I knew for sure I was going to have to go through another one of his lessons. I knew my father liked bonding and teaching me stuff, but everything he taught me was wrong. He started talking about William Floyd and how he did not want to give up his slaves; he had to. He said that while some slaves were freed and got away, others did not.

My father pointed to the water and explained, "Their bodies were thrown into the water since they tried to escape, thinking they could ever actually be free. Then our ancestors left and went to Germany and England."

He talked for the millionth time about how Hitler and his army were trying to take over, avenging William Floyd until Hitler got caught. My father finished with, "Then we came back to America to reclaim what is rightfully ours and avenge our ancestors."

I hoped he wouldn't get into the whole future lesson "NASA is working on building a life in space, and men are working on building flying cars. He really wants me to be able to join him when that time comes, blah, blah, blah."

Then he'd change the subject to the men in the post office who are making sure the right president wins. I was so tired of all the nonsense I had to listen to; I'd heard it too many times, over and over, in what felt like since I was born. Luckily, he didn't get into all of it; he only said how he wanted me to be allowed to go with him, so I must obey my orders or I'll die and get thrown into the waters. And then he finally let me soak in the many beauties of nature. I thought of all the brave heroes who lost their lives too soon but were now watching over me and everyone else on Earth. It still saddened me, though, knowing they never got a proper burial. I figured, *They would probably love to be at my grandma Daisy's grave site.*

We also went to Grandma's that weekend. I wished Aunt Greta would let Grandma take out the swimmers she had for all the little kids so we wouldn't drown, but Greta did not. I had to play in the back of the yard by myself since all the other kids were in the pool and couldn't go into the house since all the women were outside. I tried to sneak and ask my grandma to do it anyway, but Greta caught me and yelled, "Oh no, I heard you haven't even been behaving. You need to start behaving or you don't get to do certain things you want."

I spoke inside my mind, *Are you fucking stupid? Look at your kids, bitch.*

A little later, OJ had something to show me, a slingshot. He told me it's to kill the birds that go into the tree in the backyard, in the corner, a few feet away from the pool. He said that anytime I did not do what he told me to, he would kill a bird right in front of me. Then when it was time to go back inside, I heard that ear-piercing voice calling out, "Children should be seen and not heard." I obeyed, knowing I didn't have a choice, but on the way upstairs, I told her in my mind, *You stupid fucking bitch, we aren't seen or heard, and you are not my aunt, Greta! I fucking hate you, and I hope Grandma kicks you out, you dirty slut.*

Not having a choice in the matter, I had to go upstairs and do sex stuff with her nasty kids. I hated them all so much. I refused to do everything, but when OJ punched me, I listened. That night, I didn't feel like praying. I wanted to hurt but had no kitty to let cut me up, so I had to come up with another plan, a quiet one, so no one heard me.

It was so hot in the house, and I had restless legs, moving them around all over the place, rubbing them on the cold wall when I felt the wall outlet rub against my foot. I tried cutting my foot, but the trimming was too rounded off and not sharp. Remembering my mother freaking out if I tried to touch those when I was a baby, I pulled the cord that had been plugged in for our fan out a little bit and put my finger on the prong and socket, and as soon as I felt a painful vibration on my thumb and pointer, I pulled away. After a few more times of getting shocks, I was satisfied with the pain, so I closed my eyes and imagined I reunited with my dear friend, Bowie. We were about to start an army, but I didn't see anything after filling him in on everything he needed to know because I fell asleep before I even finished telling him.

That weekend, my father brought us to the neighbors, Marc and Mandy's house. Marc Jr., David, and my sister were all in the pool, so I asked Mandy if she had any swimmers, and she said no. I wanted to go in; I wished my father wasn't so cheap and would buy me a pair for home and maybe a pool too. While stuck in thought, my father came over, grabbed me from behind, threw me into the pool, and I just sank. I heard my mother screaming, and I didn't know who pulled me out, but I was so thankful they did. I wasn't expecting to get tossed in the pool, so I didn't get the chance to close my mouth or hold my breath, and I swallowed a bunch of water and couldn't breathe.

Everything was pretty much fuzzy after getting pulled out and being able to cough and breathe, but I heard my mother screaming at my father for almost drowning me. She had no idea how angry she made him, creating a scene at a gathering, or what she was in for when he got her to bed. Instead of having to hear her cry and plead for him to stop, I continued to make myself dream about Bowie helping me form an army, and I got so deep into it that I couldn't hear or see anything around me.

The next time my father had me alone, he apologized for what happened to me and admitted he shouldn't have done that, but now, whenever he could give me baths, he would teach me how to float. He told me how worried he was for me and wished I would change my mind, but since I wouldn't, Daddy would have to keep teaching me lessons to keep me alive, telling me how much he loved me and did not want me to die.

CHAPTER 22

Missing Sissy

Summer had ended, and all the kids went back to school. I was happy being alone to play with all the toys my sister never let me play with or even hold. But I knew I would miss our bonding time, especially because every summer before she started school, we would talk about all our good memories of things that happened over the summer and then get into all the good memories of our past. Sometimes, I thought we would talk about what happened with our cousins, but we didn't. We couldn't play foot wrestling before bed too much because she had to get up early, so we only played if she wasn't tired yet or on weekends. But the nights she was mad at me, if I tried to play with her, she'd kick my foot away, telling me to leave her alone and then say, "Have a bad night." But as long as she wasn't mad at me, we'd still make fun of our father, and we got to say our favorite line from the movie *The Aristocats*. One would say, "See ya in the morning, Napoleon." Then the other would respond, "Good night, Lafayette."

I missed having her to play with outside during the day, pretending I was a princess and she was my savior because my evil father locked me in my tower. She would sweep in on her white Pegasus horse and rescue me, but now I had to play and watch our funnies alone, and once she got home, I filled her in on what she missed.

Going to Grandma's was now so peaceful. I could watch my cartoons until their soap opera came on. Then I could either sit and watch it with them or play with the toys Grandma kept downstairs in a bucket for all the kids; I would do both since I liked *All My*

Children. I got irritated when OJ would know that my mother was bringing me over because he'd make Greta keep him home. Then she would say that we should be seen and not heard. It was strange because whenever Anja and my sister weren't around, OJ would be so nice to me unless I tried to tell him not to touch me like that, then he'd punch me in my arm.

Sometimes, when my mother would come upstairs to get me so we could go pick up my sister from school, OJ would beg her to let me stay while she goes and gets Ada because then she would have to come back for me and he could play with my sister for a little while. Usually, my mother would say yes, and I'd have to pretend I wanted to stay with my cousin. Before she would leave, my mother would tell OJ to make sure I did not go down those stairs by myself, and he would kindly let my mother know I was safe with him. And then, when my mother came back with my sister, we'd go to Anja's bus stop with our grandma to get her off the bus, and then it was back upstairs where we couldn't be seen or heard, and everyone was so mean to me just because I didn't want to do sex stuff.

It was completely different than the days I'd go with my mother to get my sister and we'd go straight home. On those days, my sister would tell me how her day at school was and tell me funny things that happened that day. We always got along unless I forgot to put her toys away where she had left them. Then it was an argument because I knew better than to touch her stuff. And the next school day, I'd have to hear my mother's mouth, "Make sure you put them back the way your sister did so she doesn't know you played with them, otherwise I'll have to hear her mouth and then you girls fight."

Sometimes, my mother would threaten that she wouldn't let me play with my sister's stuff anymore if I couldn't listen, but I would ignore her because I knew she'd let me anyway. My mother considered it her quiet time when her husband was at work, her oldest daughter was in school, and her youngest was content. As long as I was happy, she wouldn't have to deal with my shit fits and disrespecting her. It wasn't that I wanted to disrespect her; my father always made me be that way to her. Plus, my father told me no for everything, so I wouldn't always accept no for an answer from my mother. It wasn't as if I was asking for too much as I was a humble little girl. When she would say no, and I did have my shit fits, my mother would always say, "Ooh, I can't wait for you to start school. Then I can have peace and quiet for a few hours."

I didn't like when she said that. I didn't want to go to school, knowing I would be attending a school district where people were racist, a school district where staff and students would tell my father when I wasn't obeying the stupid German rules. I hadn't even started going to school yet, and I knew that once I was old enough, I would quit just like my mother had left school when she was old enough to. She went to the same school district as I would soon go to, and so did my father. My father got a fancy degree because he loved Adolf Hitler and William Floyd. I hated that that was where my sister had to go. I always worried about her in school. But once she'd come home, I saw how brave and strong she was to make it out alive and unharmed. Although my sister always told me good stories, I knew there were stories she kept from me because she never liked to talk about the bad times.

CHAPTER 23

All Work, No Play

Every autumn season since I could remember, I was always allowed to play in the piles of leaves my father raked up even though it made more of a mess for my sister to clean up. But this year, I had to clean up the piles with her. My father would always start raking from the front of the house to the back, so whenever he'd turn a corner and couldn't see, I'd play softly in the leaves before picking them up. My sister still yelled at me, but I told her I was cleaning the mess up too. If we fought loud enough for him to hear, our father would come and bitch that we were not to be playing; we were to be doing yard work. Then he'd rake up the pile again and complain that we were only picking up the lot of it when he wanted us to get every nook and cranny.

After he finished raking piles for us to pick up, he told my sister to pick up the other piles of leaves by herself while our father taught me how to pick up leaves, and he just kept bitching about getting every nook and cranny; it was so annoying. Sometimes I'd lie and say I had to go to the bathroom to get away from the "nook and cranny" talk for a few minutes at least. I also had to be shown how to break up the sticks, couldn't leave any little pieces behind, and how to put them in the bag so they would not tear it. I found out why my sister was always so angry that I would jump in every pile she had to pick up. Our father went crazy over nooks and crannies left behind.

Later, when we were alone in our room, I told my sister I was sorry for making messes with the leaves and how Daddy treated her for it. Ada was glad to see that I understood what it was like, and we started impersonating our father. I scrunched my face and clenched my teeth as I complained about stick bits, nooks, and crannies. My sister then scrunched her face and clenched her teeth and fists, saying, "Do you want to die early?"

We were both cracking up so much that our cranky father heard us and yelled, "Girls, don't make me have to come in there!"

Then we started making fun of him for not knowing that we were making fun of him, only we made sure to be quiet so he wouldn't come to flog our asses.

My father had grown sick and tired of me disobeying my superiors, so he quit his job to be able to keep a closer eye on me. I didn't know why he couldn't understand that I did not have superiors like him; I chose to be banned from there. I obeyed my father, didn't even look at the black people next door, and treated my mother and sister like shit when he gave the order. I had learned how to properly hail Hitler and listened to all my father's boring stories about Hitler and Floyd and all the other bad people from the beginning of time to the present day and who will be fighting in World War 3. I even learned the names of a few of the tools my father now made me help him clean.

House cleaning was my mother's chore, and my father never wanted me to help her, so I didn't have to do chores she'd ask, but now, I had to learn how to fold clothes properly. And now, he'd check my closet more frequently, and if anything were out of place, he'd pull everything out and make Ada and me stack everything properly, warning us that if it weren't to his approval, we'd get a beating. My father would not leave me alone about how to roll toilet paper around my fingers neatly instead of just crumbling it up to wipe, calling me a slob, a filthy pig, stupid, and more. Since my father's rule was only two baths a week, my mother had no choice but to listen to him. I'd get baths from her on Sundays when I was allowed to have toys in the bath, the water was at the exact temperature I liked, and I had a whole hour of playtime.

On Wednesday nights, I had to get baths from my father since my mother had to work nights so we wouldn't have to go on welfare. The water was scorching hot to the point where I had to keep pulling one leg out at a time to relieve the burn sensation on my legs and feet while my father yelled at me for being a baby, claiming the water was lukewarm, ignoring the fact that my skin was red and hot to the touch. That's when he'd tell me to sit before he made me. The burning was worse in the more sensitive areas of the body. I wasn't allowed any playtime, let alone bring in even a single toy. The only fun part was when my father taught me more about floating and holding my breath for a really long time. He would time me to see how long I could stay afloat and how long I could hold my breath. He'd tell me how proud he was of me and explain that those were important things to know in life and he had to teach me survival now because I was getting too old for him to see me naked anymore because I was no longer a baby.

He'd smile and say, "But you'll always be my baby, kit, kitty, kitten, kitten Lee."

I'd put on my cutest face as I'd pretend to lick the back of my hand and clean my forehead while I meowed and purred, making my father crack up just as much, if not more, each time I did it. I wanted those moments to last forever. I loved when he was kind and caring and playful. He was the funniest dad in the world, and I always thought, *I got his attention now. Maybe this will be when he finally follows in my path and not his anymore. Maybe he will see he is going the wrong way and turn around.*

He didn't though. He went deeper down the wrong path. Since I could talk now, I tried to tell him I was sorry for what Grandpa did to his wife and children and the abuse they suffered at the hands of my great-grandfather, whom I never met and glad I didn't have to. That only made my father angry, and he told me I was too stupid to do anything right. He yelled that I had no idea what I was talking about and I needed to go into my room to play with my dolls like a baby and get out of his face. He'd tell me I had disgusted him. He would make me go to bed without a snack because he couldn't stand to look at my face. If my sister got the chance, she'd sneak me in a snack that wasn't messy and was quick to eat so I could hide the evidence until morning when I could sneak and throw it away unnoticed.

I would stay awake every night my mother worked so that I could have her love since my father gave me his but then took it back. She'd ask what I was doing still awake, and I'd say, "I missed you. I couldn't sleep." She'd sit with me for a few minutes, and we'd talk about our evening away from each other. I'd leave out the horrible things my father did and said to me and Ada.

Sometimes, my sister would be up, but most nights, she was already asleep since it was a school night. I was thankful for the nights she was asleep because when awake, she'd tell our mother some of what our father did, and I knew what the outcome would be. Our mother would confront our father, he'd call us a liar, and then she would have to have sex with him, and I wouldn't be able to get good sleep that night.

In December 1987, I turned four years old. I was hoping some of my family could come over for cake, but my father never liked to throw us birthday parties as our cousins' parents did for them, and our mother wasn't allowed to invite anyone over. That morning, my mother had to take my sister to school, so I had to go with her since my father was still asleep. She was a little annoyed that it would have been much easier to leave me with him and then she could run the errands that she had to make and I couldn't go with her. I got upset with her for complaining about having to bring me. I was so happy that my father was still asleep and I could go with my mother without him trying to get me to stay with him. So the whole ride to my sister's school, I was such a bitch to my mother. I told her she couldn't run errands unless she took me along.

Hearing the attitude in my voice, my mother responded, "Oh yeah, we'll see about that."

My sister yelled at me, "You can't tell Mommy what to do just because it's your birthday. Stop being a brat!"

From then until we were halfway back home, my mother could no longer stand my cold-shoulder treatment toward her, and she asked, "Honey, what's the matter? Why are you so upset?"

I told her, "Because you complained about bringing me. It's my birthday. I want to be with you all day and night."

Feeling terrible, my mother responded, "Oh no, baby, I don't have a problem bringing you, it's just that when I run my errands, I can't take you because I'm getting surprises for you."

She continued how she loved spending time with me, especially on holidays and birthdays, and that it just would have been easier for her if Mommy could have taken my sister to school and run her errands so that she could come right back home to me. But since my father, who doesn't even work, was still asleep, she had to take me home, wait for him to wake up, and then be able to go before she had to pick my sister up from school. I felt horrible for treating my mother the way I did. She worked the night prior and still had to get up early to take my sister to school. Then she wouldn't have time to nap since she had surprise errands to run for me.

I apologized for being a brat to my mother while she apologized for accidentally hurting my feelings. I loved that about my mother; she always acknowledged when she did or said something wrong and would correct it, letting her children know what she meant and apologizing for upsetting us. My father never apologized for hurting our feelings; he loved upsetting his daughters and making us feel bad about ourselves, especially Ada.

When my mother and I arrived home, my father was still asleep. Not only was my mother irritated and cursing him out, but I was also, except my curse words had to be said in my brain so I wouldn't get in trouble for saying bad words. My father finally woke up, sat on his chair to eat, and watch TV, then shit, shaved, and showered for an hour, and it was almost time for my mother to pick up my sister from school. I was getting so angry at him because I knew he hated when we celebrated holidays and birthdays, so I felt like he was dragging along on purpose just so that I couldn't have a little party.

Finally, my mother could leave, and I was all alone with my dear old dad who was not so dear. He kept being especially mean to me, scrunching his face and calling me stupid. He didn't even wish me a happy birthday, something my mother did as soon as I awoke and gave me a big kiss and a squeezed hug. I went to play in my room to escape my father's terrible behavior, but he walked in not long after and teased me, telling me I was not getting a party, not even a cake.

I walked out of my room and went into the living room. My father went from the living room into the kitchen to find a snack. He said I couldn't have a snack since I liked being a slave.

Having had enough, I cried out, "Daddy, stop it! It's my special day today!"

He scrunched his face and clenched his jaw as he punished me to my room. He yelled, "Do not come out of that room until it's dinnertime, then you go right back in there!"

I ran to my room, trying hard not to cry, but the tears rolled down my cheeks. I laid down on my bed facing the wall and was glad I did because my father kept popping in to tease me a little more. By having my back facing the door, he assumed I had fallen asleep and finally left me alone. Then I must have dozed off for a bit because I woke up to my sister telling me, "Leela, time to wake up, dinner's almost done."

I woke up and used the bathroom but went straight to my room since my father didn't tell me the punishment was over. My mother came to my room to get me, and I followed her into the kitchen. Not seeing any party stuff, I figured my father wasn't kidding. We were not celebrating my birthday this year. My mother cooked my father's and my favorite plate, pork chops, and success minute rice with Campbell's pork and beans. As my father always did before sitting down to eat, he walked into the kitchen while patting his stomach and said, "Buddha, Buddha needs fooda, fooda."

Usually, I would laugh and copy him, but I didn't even look at him this time. I kept my head down so he couldn't see and rolled my eyes.

Then while my mother was serving our plates, my father sang, "Rice and beans, it's a food for the gods."

This time, he noticed I wasn't singing along and doing a cute little dance in my chair, so he sang it again. Seeing that he was looking me straight into my eyes, I just gave him a blank stare. My father waved his hand at me and said, "Eh, be a little crank."

My mother complained, "Leave her alone, Adolfi, I had to have Ada wake her up for dinner. She's probably tired."

He replied, "Yeah, yeah, sit down, shut up, and eat."

We weren't allowed to talk at the table during meals. Only when the king of the house spoke could we answer him or laugh at his jokes. And while my mother could pour us drinks, my sister and I weren't allowed to sip until we finished eating. We had to watch my father eating his meal and sipping his drink with food still being chewed in his mouth, and he'd swallow it all down. When he finished eating, my father left the table, and my mother would immediately start a conversation with her daughters, only tonight, I didn't feel like talking, so I just finished eating and went straight to my room. I heard my mother and sister say how tired I must be since I was so quiet. I tried to listen to see if they would talk about cake, but when I reached my room, I couldn't hear what was said anymore. It felt even more real that no one was celebrating my special day with me, and I curled up in the fetal position on my bed, facing the wall, and started to cry as quietly as possible.

A short while later, after I could no longer hear my mother washing dishes, my sister came in and told me I had to go into the kitchen with her.

I cried to her, "I can't, Daddy punished me when Mommy was picking you up from school."

She replied, "Oh, that's why you were so quiet."

I looked at her and said, "Yeah, I'm not allowed to celebrate my birthday." More tears came rolling down my face.

She left the room, and then my mother and sister came walking into the room. My mother sat on the bed, telling me we were celebrating my special day and told me to come into the kitchen with her. When she got into the kitchen and realized I had not followed her, she yelled out, "Ilse, come here, baby, I have a surprise for you."

I heard my father walking out of his room and went to the kitchen. My mother questioned his reason for punishing me on my birthday. As I went toward the kitchen and saw no lights except burning candles, I felt a little happy but was still sad. My father was defending himself, claiming he was only joking when he punished me, and it wasn't his fault that I couldn't take a fucking joke. I wiped away the rest of my tears and pretended I knew he was only joking and I couldn't take the joke. I knew it was an argument I would not win with him, so I let him have the score point. I was just glad to see my special day celebrated by the ones I loved most. I could never stay mad at my father for the hurtful things he had done; I blamed it on people like my grandfather and great-aunt Bertha.

That night before bed, I started thinking about the times we went to see Bowie and wondered when the nicer weather would come so we could finally visit him and his hot dog truck. I couldn't remember when was the last time we visited him; I was pretty sure we went to see him last summer, but all I could remember was all the beers I had to sip off of at family gatherings, how my cousins liked to do sex stuff to my sister and me, and how gross it was and that I wished my sister would bring it up when it wasn't happening so we could talk about it and put our feet down.

The following week was Christmas, and I was so excited because I peeked in my parents' bedroom closet and saw we were getting a kitchen set of our own. I've wanted one ever since I can remember, and my sister had wanted one before I was born. So now that I knew we were getting it, I just wanted to open it and play with it.

On Christmas Eve night, we went to my grandma's for dinner. I was so happy because I loved my grandma's cooking. After eating a lot at her house and opening our presents, we returned home and did our Christmas Eve tradition. After settling in, we had dessert in the kitchen, and then my mother told my sister and me to go inside so she could clean up and we'll watch a Christmas movie before bed.

By now, she realized that my sister was too old to believe in Santa, but my mother still had no idea that my father had killed that childhood belief of mine long ago. While my mother cleaned up in the kitchen, my sister was smart and went straight to our room to wait for our mother to finish cleaning. I was going to follow her, but my father called, "Hey, kit, come spend a few minutes with your dear old dad."

I walked over to where he was, and as I hopped up, he caught me and sat me on his lap. That's when the story began.

"Many, many years ago, way before even I was born, there was a man named St. Nicholas. He did deliver toys to children, but one Christmas Eve, there was a blizzard. There was so much wind and snow hitting him in the face in every direction. The roof he was on was so icy that he slipped off the roof, fell on the ground, and snapped his neck, dying instantly."

When my mother finished cleaning up, she came to the living room, and shortly after, my sister joined her. We sat down to watch a Christmas movie, and my father picked *Santa Claus: The Movie*. I knew why he picked it; he wanted me to see Santa in a blizzard. My father decided to have another snack and ate a chocolate ice cream bar, something that I could never refuse if offered. He was being a pig since he wasn't working and had two, but he shared one with me. My stomach warned me not to have any, but my taste buds screamed for some.

As my father offered me more, my mother pleaded, "Adolfi, enough now, no more."

Not feeling very well, I went straight to getting ready for bed after the movie ended and fell asleep before my mother came in to tuck her girls in and before Santa arrived to deliver us presents. She woke us up soon after midnight, and we began opening presents. My stomach was so upset with me I felt like I was going to puke, and my body was warm and a bit sweaty. I asked if I could use the bathroom, and my father yelled at me to hurry up because he wanted to go to bed. I went in and put my face over the toilet, but nothing. I figured maybe I had to poop instead.

My father began yelling at me to stop holding everyone up, and then my mother said, "Well, Adolfi, I told you not to keep giving her the fudge pop. She doesn't feel good."

He insisted I move it along, so I washed my hands since I touched the dirty toilet and went back into the living room. I wanted to hurry up and open my presents so I could sit on the toilet and wait for it to happen. My father smacked my hand because I was grabbing the presents, trying to find mine. I didn't understand why he wanted to take our time now when he was rushing me while I was trying to go to the bathroom. My mother saw me holding my stomach and tried to tell me to go back into the bathroom, my father whining that he was tired and not waiting anymore for me to play around in the bathroom, and he stated that I could wait until we finished opening gifts, so I tried to. My stomach had burned the whole while, but now it felt like my insides were twisting, and it automatically made me push, so I pooped all over in my pajama pants, which leaked on the floor.

My father yelled the loudest he could, "That's fucking disgusting. Get your ass in the bathroom if you want to shit. You don't shit on the fucking floor, you fucking slob."

My mother yelled at him for being the cause of my being sick, which he denied and said I shouldn't have eaten it and I could have said no. I could hear them from in the bathroom going back and forth, and he ended it by saying, "Just shut up and finish cleaning your daughter's nasty shit off the floor so we can finish." Then he yelled to me, "And you hurry up in there 'cause when you get out here, you're getting a beating for shitting yourself on the floor like you're in your mother's family's house."

After I finished wiping up and flushed, I could hear my father yelling, "Come on, let's go or you'll get another beating for making us wait."

I hurried up and washed my hands, and then my mother came in with a fresh pair of pajamas for me and helped me clean my butt and legs, noticing I didn't get it all off. After my mom finished cleaning me up, we left the bathroom where my father was waiting in the hallway. I accepted the double beating for my unavoidable actions and continued opening presents. He tried telling me to go to bed, but my mother fought back that if he didn't give me the fudge pop, I wouldn't have gotten sick, and he certainly didn't need to beat me for it. He agreed to let me finish opening presents but said I couldn't play with anything before bed.

After we finished opening presents, I went straight to my room. When my mother and sister came in, they tried to get me to play, but I didn't feel like it anyway; the double beating hurt my butt, but it hurt my heart more that my father would do that to me on Christmas while I was sick. Plus, I still wasn't feeling too well anyway. My mother tucked me in, and I faced the wall and listened to the calming sounds of her and my sister playing together. It was so relaxing that I fell right asleep. It was like listening to lullabies.

CHAPTER 24

You Have to Make Sex Noises

On Easter in 1988, my mother continued her traditions while my father wanted nothing to do with it. On the morning of Easter, while my sister and I were asleep, my mother hid the eggs we boiled the night before and set up our Easter baskets in the kitchen. Our mother excitedly told us that the Easter Bunny came once she learned we were awake. After sorting through our baskets, allowed to eat one piece of candy each before breakfast, we began our egg hunt.

Once finished, our mother took three eggs and put them aside to have with breakfast then put the remaining eggs in the fridge. While my mother cooked, my sister and I watched Easter shows in the living room until she finished, and we returned to the kitchen. While eating our breakfast, we heard our father wake up, and as soon as he came into the kitchen, the first thing he did was no surprise to any of us as he did it every year. He picked up my sister's basket, grabbed a few pieces of chocolate, put it down, and picked mine up to have some of mine as well even though right in the middle of the table sat the basket my mother always made for them to share, but he would want to save that for later. And just like every Sunday, he went into the living room, sat on his chair, and put on his church shit. That was what my mother called it, and both of her daughters agreed.

We couldn't wait to be able to go to my grandma's and not have to hear about the "true" Christian way. Hearing the nonsense on TV drove us crazy, but listening to my father preach it to us was even worse. We finished our breakfast and started getting ready to leave. Whenever I was in my father's vision, he'd call me over to him or sneak into my room if I were alone and ask, "Are you sure you don't want to stay with Daddy?" After telling him no each time, he'd get frustrated with me and say, "Fine, go be a slave at your grandmother's."

I didn't know what he was talking about; he never made sense to me, and I couldn't wait to have fun with all my cousins who visit Grandma for Easter too. I wondered, *Why would I want to stay here and listen to all this fake bullshit and lies? I'm going to get more candy from my grandma and spend time with loved ones.* Of course, I would miss my father while I was gone, and I would be glad to return home to him later when his church shit would be over.

Before we left, I caught my father digging into my Easter basket, and I decided to joke around with him. I said, "Hey, the Easter Bunny made that basket for me, fat daddy."

Before I could continue the joke and tell him the Easter Bunny made him a special basket to share with Mommy, my father scolded me, "What are you, a fucking baby? The Easter Bunny doesn't exist."

My mother heard this and got so angry with him that they began to argue. Luckily, it didn't last long since we finished getting ready, and she just wanted to leave. On the way to my grandma's, my mother apologized to my sister and me and said, "Don't pay any mind to your father. The Easter Bunny is real. He's just being a crank because he doesn't like Easter, so he thinks we shouldn't celebrate it either, but that's just too bad. He doesn't mind Easter when it comes to taking your candy."

My sister and I agreed, so I added, "That's why he's my fat daddy now."

When we got to my grandma's house, my mother was glad to be the first to arrive so she could park directly in front of the house. She hated getting there last because we'd have to park more toward the neighbor's house and walk longer to get inside. She parked right next to the mailbox, and we went inside. I saw so many little lunch-sized brown paper bags. Each bag had a name written on it. My grandma did this every year, and if someone had not visited her that day, she'd save it until she did see them. I loved to read, especially since Daddy always said that reading books stops serial killers from being able to steal kids, so I was reading the names on the bags when Uncle Otto yelled at me, accusing me of trying to take stuff that didn't belong to me. Grandma heard me tell him I was only reading the names, stepped in, and defended me, then helped me read the ones I couldn't.

Aunt Greta interrupted us by saying, "Children should be seen but not heard."

I could hear the jealousy in her voice. She hated when people defended me or my sister, and even more, she hated when someone in the family bonded with one of us, especially me. She would also get so jealous whenever someone would have a bond with my mother, forget about when someone gave us compliments. If no opportunity to break up the moment had arisen, she'd create one. She'd remember a story that was too funny to wait her turn, usually something about Anja or OJ, and having a high-pitched voice, she'd make sure the crowd's attention was on her.

I didn't have a problem going upstairs since it was Easter but only because I didn't know that even on a holiday, I'd have to do sex stuff with my cousins. Aunt Alana had come over with little Jakob and Raymond, but Raymond was older and stayed downstairs with the adults. Aunt Faith came over with her girls, but like Raymond, Jennifer was older, and she stayed downstairs. OJ kept bitching at me because I never made sex noises, and although I was starting to listen and let them do sex stuff to me, I still didn't do it right to others. I had to watch how Anja did sex stuff with my sister and Sasha while OJ did sex stuff to me, and he made little Jakob do sex stuff to me too. OJ told me to listen to the noise they made by moaning and then copy them. When I didn't do what he said, he got angry and started calling me stupid, telling me I didn't know how to be a hot chick. I had enough and yelled at him that he was lucky I did anything, explaining that I don't have to make sex noises if I didn't want to.

That's when I heard my mother yell from downstairs, "Girls, I want you to come down and spend some time with your aunts and uncles before we gotta leave."

It was music to my ears. Not only because I got out of having to do what my cousins said but also because I just wanted to spend time with Raymond and Jennifer. They never made me do anything wrong or disgusting. And whenever they were around, I was safe. The rest of my day at my grandma's was great. Everyone got along, and as each person left, my grandma reminded the kids to grab their Easter bags. When I got my Easter bag, OJ came to me and teased me because he and Anja got real presents from Grandma on Easter, not just candy. I didn't care; I appreciated the little things in life because they meant more to me.

In the car on the way home, I stared at my bag that my grandma walked to the store to buy since she didn't drive. I studied her handwriting and saw she took time to write each grandchild's name neatly and evenly on the bag. I looked inside the bag and admired how she even put hay in the bag, and the loose candies were in a sandwich bag so they wouldn't get lost in the paper bag. Then I thought about the toys she had to buy for Anja and OJ that they won't even appreciate and how they don't appreciate anything she did for them. I wished we could live with my grandma instead of Greta, Otto, and their spoiled brat children. My grandmother deserved a better life, and she was supposed to be the one to run the house, not two children who couldn't do anything right. All they knew how to do was treat her, my uncle Henry, and aunt Heidi like pieces of shit and throw garbage around the house for Grandma to clean up. When the kids unwrapped food, they threw the wrapper on the floor or shoved it in the couch cushions. When they were full and done with what they ate, they'd leave the rest for my grandmother to pick up. Sometimes, it would fall on the floor, and some would get kicked under the couch.

My father was still cranky when we returned home, but at least his church shit was over. He asked me about my time at Grandma's house, and I told him I had fun. I was good at hiding when something went wrong, so I knew I convinced my father that only good things happened. While alone in the kitchen, my father broke the chocolate bunnies into pieces and threw them all in a bowl. I hated when he did that because he always grabbed the best parts, and the bunnies were supposed to be for my sister and me. I asked him not to, and he got mad at me for being so concerned about a stupid chocolate bunny, but I didn't care about having to be a slave. He started complaining about how sex sells, women were supposed to be sexy, and people will pay big money, and how I wouldn't have to worry about any of that if I would obey simple orders and accept that I was German and needed to eat, drink, and sleep with my own kind. I didn't know what he was even talking about, and I didn't care. Talking about sex with my father was awkward enough, but hearing him talk about it right after my cousins were making me do sex stuff was another level of discomfort.

I snuck away in my brain and remembered all the good stuff that happened earlier in the day and how delicious the chocolate bunny pieces were. I wished he would leave the kitchen so my sister would join me. Knowing he was in a bad mood, she steered clear of him as best as she could in a tiny one-story, two-bedroom house. When he finally went into the living room to watch TV, my sister came to the kitchen, and my father said, "Of course, you're going right for the chocolate, you want to get fat? You fat lard of shit."

My sister wasn't even fat. She was skinny. I told her not to listen to him. He started saying that's why her clothes don't fit and she had to give them to me. My mother came out of her room and yelled at him to stop. I thought to myself, *Here goes another sleepless night. I'm gonna have to hear my father's sex noises and my mother begging him to stop.* It didn't lead to an argument, thankfully. My mother walked into the kitchen to comfort my sister, and I helped cheer her up. I pretended I was Bugs Bunny while I ate the broken piece with the candy carrot, the way Bugs Bunny eats carrots. She started laughing, but then she hurt my feelings. She said it was even funnier because with my adult teeth growing in more, I looked like Bugs Bunny with my big bucked teeth. I didn't think that was funny at all, especially when I wasn't the one who just hurt her feelings. My mother told her that was not nice and made her apologize to me; I didn't want to accept her apology though, so we just stopped talking to each other since our mother did teach us. "If you don't have anything nice to say, don't say anything at all."

CHAPTER 25

Ilse the Buck-Toothed Beaver, What's Up, Doc?

It didn't take long for my sister to jump on the opportunity to make me feel even worse about myself, not caring that our father did that to me enough. Knowing that our father treated Ada worse than me, I tried to keep my cool. But now she even had our cousins calling me Ilse the buck-toothed beaver or asking me if I wanted a carrot, reciting lines from Bugs Bunny.

OJ just loved to put his face in mine and scream, "What's up, Doc?"

The first time he got in my face, I asked him nicely not to do that. He did it again and screamed louder. Angry, I said, "Don't put your ugly freckled face in my face, your breath smells."

He punched me for it, and Anja yelled at me because she had freckles, so she insisted I was making fun of her. It didn't bother her that everyone, including her, was making fun of me. I was supposed to sit there and take it. I told my mother and grandmother about it, and they yelled at all of them, telling them if they couldn't be nice to me, stay away and go outside to play. While my sister always listened, I was shocked that Anja and OJ had listened. I was happy to be free from their torture and even more so when Grandma asked if I wanted to watch my funnies. She put on Looney Tunes for me, and when a Bugs Bunny cartoon came on, I laughed while thinking how the next time OJ calls me Bugs Bunny, I would call him Elmer Fudd.

Later, when my aunt Greta made me play with the kids, OJ started talking to me like Bugs Bunny, so I started reciting lines from Elmer Fudd, telling him he looked just like that weird little man who had nothing better to do than hunt rabbits and wear the same clothes every day.

It didn't offend OJ as he replied, "I'd love to have a gun and hunt animals."

They all started teasing my buck teeth again, so I called my sister a fat lard of shit. It was her fault that I was going through this anyway. OJ ran into the house, and I heard my mother yell from the kitchen window, "Ilse Leigh, get your ass in this house, *right now*!"

Knowing I was in big trouble, I slowly walked toward the house. OJ ran back by me and followed me to let me know he even told my mother I cursed. When I got inside, my mother was screaming at me about how I knew that my father was always teasing Ada and I shouldn't act like that asshole father of mine. I tried defending myself, letting my mother know that they started it by teasing me.

She snapped back, "And I'm finishing it! Enough, no more picking on each other, or I'll start smacking."

As my mother made me angry at her, I replied, "Go ahead, your smacks tickle."

My grandmother nicely said, "Lee Lee, don't talk back to your mother, yous girls gotta stick by each other."

Aunt Greta then had to put in her two cents, "Oh yeah, you like cursing and talking back to your mother?" She walked into the bathroom and then came into the living room and handed my mother a white bar of soap. "Put this in her mouth, that'll teach her to curse."

Hoping my mother would tell her sister off and not do what she suggested, I was surprised to see my mother walking toward me, and she put the soap in my mouth, turned the bar of soap around a bit, and then pulled it out and said, "Now go apologize to your sister. And from now on, if she picks on you, you don't do the same. You come and tell me, and I will correct her."

The next time we visited other houses, some of our other cousins teased my buck teeth too. At Aunt Faith's, it would be my sister and Sasha. Jennifer always defended me, then she told me how cute I looked with my adult teeth. But when Jennifer wasn't there, I had to tell my mother about them if they wouldn't stop.

While visiting Aunt Alana and Uncle Jakob's house, it would be my sister and little Jakob. Sometimes, Raymond would pick on me a little about it, but he always told me he was only kidding, would never hurt me, or let anyone else hurt me.

I told him, "That's why you're my favorite cousin, you and Jennifer."

If his brother and my sister didn't stop teasing me, he'd step up and tell them that was enough, just like our cousin Jennifer did for me. They were my heroes, and I made sure they knew it. I always told them how much I loved them and appreciated their protection. Jennifer always said that her brothers protect me too, and I'd say, "Yeah, I know, but you and Raymond are my favorite."

I was forbidden to tell her that her brothers followed our family's German rules. Whether they wanted to protect me or not, it was against the rules, so they couldn't.

Summertime came quickly, and the kids were out of school until September. Holiday breaks were long enough, but having to deal with my cousins and my sister repeatedly teasing my buck teeth for the next two months was not something I was looking forward to. With my father out of work, my mother would take us there almost every day. I loved visiting my grandma, aunt Heidi, and uncle Henry, but I could not live through Anja, OJ, and my sister cornering me, teasing me, pointing in my face, or putting their face in mine. The only time they were nice to me was when they wanted me to let them do sex stuff to me or if an adult was around, other than their parents, since they let their kids behave that way.

I loved the days we would hang out at Aunt Faith's house because even though Sasha was such a pain in my ass, it was more peaceful there and clean because my aunt Faith raised her children to be clean. The only time it got noisy and a little crazy was when my aunt Faith or uncle Jakob found out their boys were doing illegal things and getting themselves into trouble. Plus, at least Sasha and my sister didn't constantly pick on me; we played together at times the way cousins should play together. And when Sasha was behaving, she was funny and cool. That's how it was at Aunt Alana's house too, but I got along with little Jakob way more than Sasha. Going to Aunt Betty's, I never got teased, only playful teasing, and no one made me feel bad about my teeth. If Anja and OJ were over, they weren't allowed to tease me, or they would get yelled at by so many adults. And none of the kids liked being yelled at by Aunt Betty; she was considered the head honcho in the family, the one everyone went to when there were issues between family members.

Aunt Betty would work their differences out for them since they couldn't do it themselves. But anytime it was a family gathering where too many drunk people were together and disagreed, a screaming match would turn into a fistfight. The people fighting didn't even care to look if children were around either; they'd fight over them if the kid were in the wrong place at the wrong time. You would hear kids crying and screaming and see mothers grabbing their children and leaving, mine being one of the smart ones who didn't want to stick around. If my father were with us, he'd say how my mother's family was nothing but drunks and animals, and he did not want her bringing us over there anymore. Other than that and the visits when I caught my little cousins doing sex stuff to each other and then had to watch them get their asses beat, I loved being there because no one ever did anything sexual to me. And I was treated with respect by the kids and adults. Except for Uncle Wilheim, he ignored me like I wasn't even there, just how I liked it to be.

At home, my sister would only tease me about my buck teeth if she were angry with me or when our father told her to. But he made her tease me for being stupid more than being a buck-toothed beaver. He also got my sister back for insisting I looked like a Looney Tunes character; he told my sister that she was the Wile E. Coyote and I was the Road Runner. Or, of course, he'd insist she looked like Porky Pig. Then because Greyhound got stronger and broke the chain links setting her free, running around the whole yard, and he could not catch her, he made my mother come out to help him. Greyhound knew my mother would never hurt her, so she decided to play with my mother and charged at her. Greyhound was running so fast, and my mother was afraid she'd break her skinny legs if she hit them head-on, so she moved over. Greyhound then ran into the metal bumper of the family car, headfirst. Before my mother could get to her to be sure she wasn't hurt, the doggy shook her head from side to side a few times and then continued running for her freedom.

My mother, sister, and I thought it was the cutest thing and couldn't help but laugh and stare in amazement at our pup's speed. Not that she was a puppy anymore, but we all called her our pup, even my father did when he wasn't in the mood to give out beatings. My father yelled at my mother for playing with the damn dog instead of helping and being useful in her life for once, so my mother did. She went back inside the house to give him his space, telling my sister and me to follow. My father told my sister she could go since she was too fat to run, like Porky Pig, and I had to stay with him to help catch Greyhound since she always came to me when I called her. I begged him not to make me do that to her, and he started calling me a stupid buck-toothed beaver, asking if I wanted a carrot, and then said, "Oh yeah, I forgot you don't eat carrots, you only eat junk food."

My father hid while I stood not far from him, and I had to get her to come to me for love. When she did, I looked her in the eyes and whispered, "I'm so sorry, Greyhound, Daddy made me trick you."

My father grabbed her by the collar and dragged her to where no one could see him flog her ass, and he put her on a bigger chain to bathe her, teasing her for being afraid of the water. He strongly suggested she toughen up and act more like Sweety across the street. I had to help him give her a bath since my mother was inside.

CHAPTER 26

Hand-Me-Downs

Excited that I got more hand-me-down clothing from my sister, I picked the ones I liked so my mother could make a donation bag for the Salvation Army. This summer, I got to wear clothes I already had. I was now big enough to fit in the clothes that matched the clothes I had, which I grew out of because now my sister had grown out of hers. One clothing item was black spandex shorts with a black skirt attached, and on the skirt was a picture of Minnie Mouse. Another favorite was the bathing suit bikini we had. It was a bathing suit that had holes, showing the stomach and back with ties on the sides. Each part was a different fluorescent color, pink, green, yellow, purple, and blue. I also got some nightgown pajamas and some shorts and T-shirts, but the Minnie shorts skirt and the bathing suit bikini were what I loved most.

When it came time to pick out the clothes that hung in the closet, the only thing that would fit me was Ada's yellow dress with black polka dots. When my mother bought that one and a matching one for me, my sister and I loved them; we both looked so good in that dress. I liked how I looked in it, but it matched my sister better because she had blonde hair and blue eyes. Knowing how much I loved that dress, my mother was confused when she asked if I wanted to keep or donate it, and I said donate it. I had to think fast when she asked why, so I said I didn't like polka dots. The real reason was that that dress reminded me of when my father beat us with belts in the discipline room at Great-Aunt Bertha's house; my sister got beat for our mother dressing us alike. I could remember hearing Bertha complaining about it to my father. I was so glad we did not have to go there anymore, but I missed my uncle Hans and aunt Maple.

When I tried everything on, I picked to keep a few things, including the shorts and the bathing suit; they were a little too big for me, so I whined like a baby when my mother suggested we put them away until next summer. She said we could use a ponytail on the shorts, and she'd try to tie the bathing suit tighter.

When my father saw me in the shorts with a ponytail tied off to the side, he laughed at how cute I looked and then teased my sister, saying, "See, I told you you're getting to be a fat lard of shit, your sister doesn't even fit in them yet, and you're too fat for them."

I felt horrible for my sister and wished I let my mother put them away until they fit me. I didn't follow her to our room because I didn't want our father to yell at me for going and comforting her, but as soon as I got the chance, I went into the room and tried telling her that she was not fat and not to listen to him.

I hoped she would play with me, but when I asked, she said, "I can't 'cause I'm too fat. Your father will probably yell at me since you're skinny."

I replied, "He's our father, and just don't listen to him when he's in a bad mood."

She told me to shut up and leave her alone before she punched me. Then she added, "And, no...he's not my father."

When my mother took out our kiddie pool and I was eager to wear the bathing suit, my sister teased me about not knowing how to swim and being too scared to go in a big pool without something to make me float.

She said, "You know you could easily convince Adolfi to buy us a big pool, so it's your fault why we don't have one."

I told her not to call our father by his real name and then tried to explain that it was not like that. She didn't know that for our father to get us a big pool, I would have to do terrible things to her or our mother. Instead of telling my sister the truth, I said Daddy would know it was for her since I was fine with the kiddie pool and not having a big one, so I knew he wouldn't buy it anyway. We started arguing, and she told me to get inside and take the bathing suit off because I was no longer allowed to have it.

Hearing us fight back and forth, my mother came to us and yelled, "What's the problem here, girls?"

As we tried telling her our side of the story and our mother had to tell us one at a time, she let Ada tell her side first. My sister told her about the pool situation, and she wasn't happy when my mother told her, "Maybe one day we'll get a big pool, but your sister feels safer in the kiddie pool, and you know your father's too cheap to buy it anyway. He won't even buy floats for your sister."

Then I told my mother how Ada told me I couldn't keep her old clothes, so my mother told her she couldn't give something to someone and then take it back. Feeling like no parent was on her side while both were on my side, my sister was mad at me for the whole rest of the day and even at bedtime. It wasn't until the next day, after waking up a bit, that my sister finally spoke to me again. I was so glad she wasn't mad at me anymore. I loved her more than she could ever know.

Since Anja grew out of her Strawberry Shortcake bike and had gotten quite a few new ones, she told me that when I'm ready to learn how to ride a bike, I could have it; she knew how much I loved Strawberry Shortcake, and my grandma was tired of having all their old bikes in the basement collecting dust and spiderwebs. While my grandmother intended to give the bike to me, my father said no because I refused to ride a bike without training wheels. He had been teasing me for a while now because when my sister was a baby, someone gave her a little red tricycle with a seat and two steps in the back. I loved riding that since you could sit and ride or stand on the steps and push yourself. Even better, my sister and I used to play on it together all the time before she got a hand-me-down bike.

While OJ had to show Uncle Adolfi the new bike he got, we all went to the basement. My sister was kind to me, and she told me that riding a bike was so easy to learn, suggesting she'll help me. I decided I wanted to learn how to ride the bike without training wheels. I tried getting my father's attention, but he was busy playing with OJ.

After getting Daddy's attention, he yelled at me for interrupting him then angrily asked, "What do you want?"

I answered, "I wanted to tell you I'm ready to learn how to ride a bike without training wheels."

He responded, "Oh, well, isn't that nice?"

Then he told me I still couldn't have the bike until I obeyed him. I didn't know what he meant. I always abided by his rules, and I took every form of disciplinary action so much so that when my father said get over here and get your beating, I was there in the flick of a switch, waiting to get my discipline, hold a phone book in the corner, stood in front of his chair so he could beat my ass over and over to the point it felt like my ass cheeks were on fire.

Anja and OJ were well aware of my obedience as my sister had confided in them about us having to get our beatings by our father. But still, they were on my father's side, telling me to start obeying. Not long after, we went back into the house. All the kids had to be seen and not heard since Greta and Otto demanded it. When I gave attitude and tried to refuse to listen to them, Anja and OJ reminded me I wouldn't get the bike. I was so confused about what that had to do with getting the bike, but I didn't want to fight with them, so I listened to them. I thought how if my father found out that I was doing sex stuff, and with blood relatives too, he'd surely beat the living shit out of me. It scared me to think of what he might do, and if he caught my sister, he'd probably try to take her out of this world since he brought her into it.

To my surprise, my father had a change of heart, and the Strawberry Shortcake bike was mine to take home. I was so happy to have Anja's old bicycle, except it annoyed me when she would say she would take her bike back if I didn't do what she and her brother said, and at home, my father would threaten to give the bike away. He tried to teach me how to ride my bike, and since I couldn't follow every step he taught me—pedaling, holding the handlebars, making turns—the bike would turn on its own, and I fell right off every time. It didn't help that I didn't know where I was supposed to be looking, and the bike was moving so fast because my father ran with me and then just let me go.

As my father's patience had always run very thin, he got angry and yelled at me, "Ah, how could you be so stupid that you can't even ride a bike and you're gonna be five years old? Gimme that fucking thing, I'll give it back."

I was a little upset because the pedals hit me in my legs and I got hurt. My father didn't even care if I was okay, but at least I had some bruises to push on until they healed. He wound up putting the bike in the basement, and I wasn't allowed to ride it again until I wasn't so stupid. But at times, when I wasn't even doing anything wrong and had to get disciplined for it, my father would also threaten to take the bike away if I didn't start obeying my superior's demands. He had me to the point that I didn't care whether or not I ever had a bike. I wished I had the guts to tell him to take it away already.

While my father usually preferred I'd get hand-me-down clothing so that he didn't have to waste money on new clothes when I didn't even go to school yet, there were limits. We'd always take a family drive to the Salvation Army once my mother had finished packing up all the clothes to donate. We weren't allowed to get out of the car, though; he would throw the bags into the clothing drop bins, and sometimes, he would go inside for a little while. Wishing he'd hurry up, my sister and I would get bored, and my mother would play games like picking a number or color or I spy. I always hoped he'd come out with someone's hand-me-downs for us, but he didn't. And after asking the first time if he could get me something, I knew not to ask again. He was so angry at me for wanting clothing from a secondhand store. I didn't see what was different from family passing down their stuff to me, but I sadly said, "Okay, fine."

My father would yell at me when he'd bring home what he claimed to be rags to my mother, but when we were in the basement, my father would pull them out of the bag they were in and would fill the holes he made in the basement floor, I would see some nice stuff that might fit me or my sister or my mother. I would ask him, "Please, can I just have that one? It's so pretty."

He would make his angry, scrunchy face and ask, "What the fuck do you want slaves' clothing for? You need to concentrate and see what I'm doing so that this doesn't happen to you."

He went on and on about his racist ways and how women and children were slaves, blah, blah, blah. I acted like I was paying attention to every word, but I went to my happy place, and he caught me. I had to go back upstairs, and when he finished, I had to be ready for my discipline. If my mother were home at the time, we'd have to go in his room and have father-daughter time as he'd tickle me to what felt like was going to be my death. If she was at work, I'd get beat or he'd make me hold the phone book.

CHAPTER 27

Like King David, Daddy Has Many Wives

My father liked to think of himself as the historical King David who had eight wives. Sometimes, he'd joke around and call himself King David. My mother would say, "Yeah, you're royal alright, a royal pain in my ass." Neither she nor my sister would laugh at his joke. I always felt sorry for my dad when they didn't laugh, and I knew I would be hurt if I told a joke and no one laughed, so I laughed at every joke he shared with us unless I was upset with him or if it was a joke that could hurt someone's feelings. Being used to having a fan who loved his jokes, when he told one I found offensive and didn't laugh, my father would call me stupid for not getting the point of it, and I would respond in my brain, *No, I got the joke, it was a stupid fucking joke.*

In one father-daughter bonding session, my father decided to tell me a secret he had been hiding from me. He looked me straight in my eyes and said, "Like King David, Daddy also has many wives. Of course, not legal marriage. I'm only legally married to your mother. But back in time, men were allowed to marry multiple women. They could even all live under the same roof."

He explained how the Republicans were trying to take complete control over America so it can be that way again, so they have to get the Democrats out of office. He told me about Prince Phillip being Queen Elizabeth's slave and how if I changed my mind about being a slave, I could be like her. Not the whole queen of England part but the superiority and the riches, tons of money I wouldn't know what to do with and all the jewelry I wanted. My father also shared that the queen's son, Prince Charles, was superior, and he had more wives than Princess Diana. He told me that Prince Charles had more children than she or the public knew of, but his son, William, was the heir to the throne.

My father explained that Harry was only allowed royal treatment because the people knew of his birth, and the royals couldn't risk getting exposed. He'd say, "But, man, I'd love to just smack the freckles right off his ugly little face."

I didn't think Prince Harry was ugly at all. I had a bit of a crush on him and wondered what it would be like to be a real princess. I knew my father said he wasn't a real prince, but I also knew he talked crap about people he didn't like, whether he knew them or not. If his brother is a prince, Harry is a prince. My father then informed me that I had more siblings than I knew about, and he stressed that they would have to die if I told anyone anything he told me. Then my dear old dad said the only reason he shared secrets with me was that Daddy wanted the best for his princess and maybe telling me would get me to open my eyes and see I needed to start following his path.

He began bitching about Princess Diana and how she thought she could make changes to the monarchy. He especially hated how she made slaves believe they had a purpose in life other than serving their masters. My father said that she was a fucking slave herself, and she needed to shut her slut mouth and obey her master, Prince Charles. He added that if Diana didn't cut the shit or if she were to get caught committing adultery, she would have to die.

That night, I cried before bed, and my sister got mad at me for crying for no reason again. I wished I could tell her I had just found out we had other siblings and that Daddy said they'd die if I told. I wanted to tell her everything she wasn't allowed to know from our lives to the royals in England. My sister didn't like to keep my secrets as she always had to tell Anja and OJ so they could all make fun of me. I couldn't risk her telling someone because one of our siblings would die. Maybe even her. I decided it was best to let her think I was crying for no reason. I would take her being annoyed with me and yelling at me over her never being around me again.

My father never missed an opportunity to make my mother feel less about herself while he would comment about other women on TV. While I never liked that he did, it now disgusted me, knowing he had other women besides my mother. He would say terrible things like, "Whoa, look at the ass and tits on that one. Don't you wish you could look like that, Rosewitha?" or "Why don't you have a body like that?" He would take it further and mention, "The things I would do to her."

The fact that he had been talking about a famous person, who, to my mother's knowledge, my father would never even meet, she would respond with things like, "Why would she want you, ya deaf bastard?" or "I wish she'd take you away from me, then I don't have to put up with your shit anymore."

But I knew it made my mother self-conscious about herself; her facial expressions said it all. Plus, I felt her pain. Her husband should never feel those ways about any woman but his wife. I decided I needed to figure out how to convince my father to let me learn how to read his atlas map book and the other maps he always had in the car. Then I could learn how to travel, and once I would be old enough, I could warn Princess Diana and Prince Harry, and they could help me build an army.

I wanted to ask my father why we hadn't seen Bowie, but he was always in a bad mood, so I never found a good time to ask if we could visit the Indian man. Only my father could say when we could speak about someone that wasn't German unless it were to say hurtful, racist things about them.

One sunny day, while my mother was hanging clothes on the line outside that my father made with his spare rope from the basement, my sister didn't want me near her because she was tired of me always wanting to be the princess as she had to be my savior, so I was pacing back and forth, thinking of what to say to my father when he asked why I wanted to learn how to read a map. I walked past Greyhound a few times; she became a playful pup and kept trying to grab onto my shorts. I swatted her away each time and explained that I needed to concentrate, but she wasn't listening. My shorts were another one of my favorites, loose fit with a spandex waist, and they were light pink with white hearts all over them. I stopped passing Greyhound, and she did a cute little stance, so I laughed and turned around to walk the other way when she ran over and grabbed onto my shorts with her mouth then proceeded to drag me, pulling me from behind so that I couldn't see where she was taking me.

At first, I was laughing because she was so cute, and I loved when she was a playful pup. The only problem was she got a little too crazy, and her jog turned into running. My laughter became cries for help, and that was when my mother looked back and saw what our pup was up to. My sister laughed once she saw while my mother began chasing after us, yelling, "Greyhound, let go, now!"

I started laughing while I was crying because it was pretty funny. When Greyhound finally let me go, my mother rushed over to be sure I wasn't hurt. I loved how my mother was such a worrywart. It made me know she cared about me. And it sort of made up for my father's lack of concern for his children's well-being. Later, when I finally got a bonding moment with my father, I brought up maps, and without questioning why, he went and got the atlas one. He let me see it and talked to me about it, and I started asking questions about how to read it. He started tickling me a lot. I was growing tired of not knowing how to get places, and I couldn't understand why he wouldn't allow me to learn. I hated how he always took different ways to one location and said how far things were in miles.

My mother always said how far places were in time. I knew the distance in time because my mother would say, "We'll be at your grandmother's in less than ten minutes." Ten minutes was how long I had to hold up a phone book without lowering my arms, so that was easy to know. Plus, my sister taught me time after she learned about it. I couldn't tell time on a clock unless it was a digital clock. My sister tried teaching me, but it was confusing and frustrating, so I would pick a fight with her so that she would stop trying to get me to be smart like her; as far as I was concerned, I was stupid.

CHAPTER 28

Fat Daddy Got a Job

My mother had been arguing with my father for a while to get a job. She'd tell him there was no reason why he should even be out of work, especially for this long. He had ignored her every time until he decided it was time to get back out there and land a job. Not long after looking, he got hired at his new job. He told me that my fat daddy got a job already unlike my mother who had to apply for multiple jobs before someone decided to hire her. He said it was because he had a diploma and my mother did not since she was stupid. I hated when he spoke about her like that. My mother was far from it; at least she knew the true meaning of life unlike my father who got a bachelor's degree. Not only that, but my father knew that my mother didn't exactly have the choice to graduate as she had to start contributing to the household. She was tired of breaking the law to have new clothes and other necessary items one needs, and she was old enough to work, so she got a job to help her mother out and to start earning a living.

I was glad I didn't have to hear all the stories I'd wished I never had to listen to as much as when my father was out of work. He'd get up early in the morning to leave for work. My sister had gone back to school again, so now it was just my mommy and me from around eight thirty or so whenever it was that my sister's bus picked her up at the bus stop. Then later, we'd leave to get my sister off the bus around three thirty, give or take some minutes. My sister would enjoy a father-free house until about five thirty/six o'clock. My mother would make sure dinner was ready, and as soon as he'd arrive, she'd kiss her family goodbye and leave for work. Both of their jobs were Monday through Friday, so on weekends, we felt trapped and longed for Monday so that we didn't have to be around our father/husband all day for five days. Life was as great as it could get for the three of us.

My father became less of a crank, or at least it seemed that way since he was out of the house a lot now. But he started doing good things, and I wondered if getting a good job was all he needed. One weekend while he said he'd be busy in the basement and we could not interrupt his concentration, he made a wooden toy box for my sister and my toys. It was big, and he even made a lid for it. Then when my sister wasn't in the room, I opened the lid, got inside the toy box, covered myself with toys, and closed the lid. She wasn't coming, and whenever I would hide on someone, for some odd reason, it always made me feel like I had to pee. I opened the lid to yell "Sissy!" and then hurried and closed it again. I dug my way to the bottom, knowing she'll probably only move some toys. She didn't see me and knew I must be playing hide-and-seek. She walked near me and lifted the lid on the toy box. She moved a few toys around, and then she closed the lid. I waited a few seconds, uncovered the toy box before jumping up, and screamed, "Roar!"

She screeched, "Oh my God." She was so confused about how she even moved some toys but didn't see me.

On another day, my father let me go out in the backyard while he did some yard work. My sister stayed inside with our mother. He went to go into the basement, so I started to follow him, thinking maybe he's got another surprise for us down there, and he yelled at me to get in the house. I went inside with an upset face, and my mother asked what was wrong.

I told her, "Daddy yelled at me to come back inside."

My sister said, "That's why I don't go out there with him anymore unless he makes me."

My mother kindly said, "Stay in here with us. He's probably got another bug up his ass."

My father came storming into the house through the back door and complained to my mother that there was a flood in the basement, and knowing our slum landlord, he wasn't going to come and fix it, so my father needed my mother to keep my sister and me inside the house. I saw my father go into the basement, and since his pants weren't wet, I asked how that was. He yelled at me to mind my fucking business and go play with my dolls, and I could hear him tell my mother that he had to stop me from running into the basement, and she replied, "So that's why she came inside with a puss on her face."

My father informed my mother that he would be making a lot of noise because he would have to make holes in the basement floor so the water could drain out and then he'd fill them with rags and re-cement the holes. He briefly bitched about how he wished the landlord would get to the house and fix the shit as he walked back outside. My mother didn't mind since the longer he stayed in the basement, the more time we had for peace.

One evening, when my father returned home from wherever he had gone, I was excited to see that he had a cat with him. I figured he felt sorry for lying about me and wanted to make it up to me. This cat was full-grown, and she was a multicolored cat with the markings of a tiger. My father pointed out how she always looked mad, so we named her Maddy. My mother told my father that she didn't want another cat that he won't let stay inside because it'll probably run away like the last one. My sister and I begged my mother to allow us to keep her, showing off how cute the cat was and how she needed a home.

After some convincing, my mother agreed we could keep her. The first chance I got alone with Maddy, I made her cut up with me and was a little upset to learn that she wasn't as playful as White Tiperella was. She would only attack me a little bit, and she barely even left a mark. I decided that maybe it was better that way anyway because I could never control myself, and I'd let my kitty attack me too much. After some time of teaching her how to play like the cat I used to have, Maddy began hiding under the couch, waiting for me to run by so she could sneak up behind me, grab the back of my legs, and bite. Her already mad face was too cute once her ears went back, and her eyes got all crazy. But unlike White Tiperella, Maddy refused to lay on her back so I could scratch her belly. That was always how I got White Tiperella to scratch up my arms. While Maddy would lie on her back and look so cute and playful, as soon as I would try to put my hand near her belly, she'd get up and run. I had to settle for biting my legs only.

Greyhound didn't get her way with Maddy either. My playful pup loved to think that kitties were her babies, but Maddy wouldn't have it as she'd smack Greyhound and run away from her as she did to me. Other than that, they got along well. Maddy loved to attack Greyhound's wagging tail, and they loved to snuggle up with each other, especially when one of them got a beating. When my father noticed them snuggling, he'd get angry and shoo the cat away from the dog then yell at them for babying each other when they recently got disciplined.

CHAPTER 29

Finally Five but Still Stupid

It felt comforting when it was already my favorite season, autumn. Even though I had to hear my father keep it up about the damn stick bits and getting every nook and cranny, I still loved doing yard work for some reason. The bugs I saw didn't bother me since I had a pair of gloves on. I felt a sense of freedom and like I was bonding with Mother Nature. I wondered if Mother Nature was God's wife or his mother. I wanted to ask my father, but he didn't want to be bothered with stupid questions; he only wanted to finish yard work.

When my mother called us in for lunch, I asked her. She laughed and said Mother Nature is Earth, and God created Earth.

I replied, "So she's God's daughter?"

She laughed harder and said, "Oh, I don't know, but that's a good question."

Her response made me feel smart since only smart people ask good questions. But as soon as lunch was over, my sister and I were with our father and him calling Ada a fat lard of shit and me stupid. He never let us have fun and enjoy the beauty of nature as he acted as if something terrible would happen if we did not get the whole yard done in a day; it was so annoying. I wished I could be inside with my mother and learn how to do household chores. But my father always told me not to, so any time my mother would ask for help inside the house, I told her I was too tired, and I'd go in my room and play with my toys or I'd have her put on a movie for me and I'd lay on the couch. My sister would always help her, and she'd complain to our mother that I'll help our father but not our mother.

My mother would say, "That's alright, wait until the next time she wants something from me."

If my sister walked by or into the bedroom and saw me playing, she'd tell on me and try to get me in trouble. My mother would remind her that it was much easier to get things done without me getting in the way. I agreed with her because she was cranky and yelled at me for making her job harder when I was chasing the dog or cat around.

To test my mother and see if she would get me something the next time I asked, I'd sometimes wait for her to be in a better mood and then ask if she could walk us up to the candy store on Warlock Rd. She'd agree to take us for a nice little walk and let us pick out a few things.

She'd say, "I might as well grab a pack of cigarettes while we're there." She used to smoke Newport before I was born, but she switched to Salem Menthol lights.

*****

Thanksgiving wasn't too bad other than being forced to watch *March of the Wooden Soldiers* again. I hated Laurel and Hardy with a passion, especially Hardy with his wannabe Hitler mustache. I'd rather watch The Three Stooges, who at least were sometimes funny. But every year, my father would be excited to watch it. He'd say, "Hey, kit, guess what Daddy's watching! C'mon, come sit on your fat daddy's lap and watch it with me."

He acted like I loved the movie as he did when I never even showed interest in it. It wasn't that I'd have to get beat for not watching it like scary movies, but it was a holiday, and it was the only time he enjoyed the holiday, so I wanted to share the moment of joy with him. As my father would laugh at the parts he found funny, I would laugh with him. When someone would do something stupid, he would crack up and ask, "Did you see that, kitten? That was fucking stupid." To which I would laugh and respond "Yeah" even though I hadn't seen it.

Since he was calling them names, I decided to try it out and allow myself to have fun until the boring movie ended. I began teasing Laurel for having a long face and Hardy for being a fat Hitler wannabe. While I was sure that would have made him laugh, it didn't. Instead, he yelled at me to be quiet, watch the movie, or play with my toys in my room. Since I wanted nothing more than to spend quality time with my father on my favorite holiday, I stayed quiet and only laughed when he laughed and agreed with his comments.

For my birthday this year, my father was in a much better mood than he had been the year prior. He didn't punish or beat me, but one of his comments felt just as painful when I mentioned that I was finally five and getting smarter.

My father responded with, "Finally five but still stupid."

My mother began to defend me, but I convinced her he was only joking and didn't hurt my feelings so I could avoid having to either hear him make her have sex before bed or him lying and saying I did something wrong so that he could beat me for it. I just wanted to get through my birthday without feeling like I wished I wasn't born. Something that my sister would always say when feeling down and depressed was that she hoped our father would take her out of this world. It would hurt to hear those words come out of her mouth, but I understood and felt the same way about myself many times. I wanted to die so the constant pain and hurt would stop. But I told my sister she couldn't die because Mommy and I would miss her too much.

This year on my birthday, my sister didn't want to hear what I had to say to cheer her up. She was upset and felt like everyone loved me more than she. Our father had been teasing her, saying she was getting too fat to have my cake and other mean, uncalled-for comments. I was so angry with him for it. I loved sharing my special day with my sister, but our father made it so she didn't want to be around me.

When I got the command to call my sister a fat lard of shit, I looked my father straight in his eyes and said, "No, she's not even fat, you are fat, Daddy."

He waved his hand toward me and replied, "Eh, what do you know? You're too stupid."

And all the while, my mother yelled, "Cut it out, Adolfi!" or "Enough now. Leave her alone. She's not fat, you are ya fat fuck. And will you stop calling Ilse stupid? She's not stupid."

But other than that, I had a good birthday and was happy to be another year older and another year closer to preparing for World War 3. I couldn't wait to stop all the nonsense and make all the evil people leave the United States and go to their country.

Christmas was great this year, with both of our parents working. My mother went crazy and got us the most she ever had. We got more coloring and reading books than just one each. I got my favorite book, *Count the Puppies*. We each got a Cabbage Patch doll, which I could not stop picking up and smelling. We got Barbie dolls, not the cheap fake Barbie either, the real Barbie. There were so many presents to open; I thought I had been dreaming.

My father complained the whole time that my mother wasted too much money. My mother would defend herself and remind him that it was her money that she was spending on their children after putting in her contribution to the household necessities. I was getting fed up with my father's bullshit and stayed close to my sister so we could speak and our father couldn't hear. We talked about our mother being right while our father was wrong. I told my sister I wished he would go into the bedroom and leave us be. She said she hoped he would leave the house and never come back. I didn't like that she took it that far, but I didn't want our bonding moment to end so quickly, so I just changed the subject and talked about the smell of our Cabbage Patch dolls. She loved the smell of them too.

While waiting for our father to stop picking fights with our mother so that we could continue to open our presents, my sister and I played together with what we'd already opened. We knew better than to grab one to open ourselves; we had to wait for someone to pass us a gift. One present I was not happy to receive was a My

Buddy doll. I wanted one when they first came out, but we were never allowed to have toys that just came out. We had to wait a few years for the toy to go down in price. Then when the creator of My Buddy made Kid Sister, I wanted the My Buddy doll, and I wanted Ada to get Kid Sister. I didn't mind having a boy doll since I was supposed to be born a boy. I felt my sister was born the way she was supposed to be, a girl, so she deserved the girl doll. But now I was used to not having either, plus my father said we weren't allowed to have boy dolls. If we wanted to play where there were girl and boy dolls, we'd pretend some girls were boys. Ada would tie their hair up to make it shorter, and we'd put baggy clothing on them.

It had been a few months since OJ had suggested I ask for a My Buddy doll. He said he'd even ask my father to get it for me. OJ had me so annoyed with his suggestion turning into a demand. One day, he asked, "Uncle Adolfi, can you get Ilse a My Buddy doll for her birthday or Christmas? She's always wanted one since they came out, and she's been being good."

I jumped into the conversation and said, "No, Daddy, I want Kid Sister. I don't want My Buddy anymore."

My father smiled and said, "Yeah, that's nice. Now get outta here, kids, ya bother me." He always played around with us like that, but also he hated being asked, especially by a kid, to waste his money.

When OJ told Anja their uncle's answer, she told him he should have gone to Aunt Rosewitha, reminding OJ that our mother was the one who bought us our presents, not our father. OJ ran up to my mother and asked her the same question, and I asked my question about getting Kid Sister instead. I didn't know what OJ's problem was why he wanted me to have that damn doll in the first place. He'd rather I have nothing, but suddenly, he was adamant about me getting a toy I didn't want.

Before we left my grandmother's that day, I learned that the My Buddy doll was for me to practice on. My cousins thought I would get practice at home so I could perform with them. At first, they had wanted my sister to teach me things at home, but she told them, "Hell no, I am not touching my sister."

So when opening the My Buddy doll this Christmas, I put on a fake smile and thanked my mother since I knew she bought it for me or at least I thought she did. My father stepped in to take the credit for getting me that present. It was hard to fake another smile for him. I wasn't willing to give him credit, but I did just so as not to offend him, and I said, "Thanks, Daddy."

CHAPTER 30

I Know You're Not Practicing

A few months passed, and I had to watch *Child's Play*. It was so scary that I stayed up most of the night watching My Buddy doll to make sure he didn't come to life and kill my sister and me. It was starting to freak me out that My Buddy had a lot of similarities to the Chucky doll. I knew I wouldn't be able to get rid of it. My father would notice it was missing. I put it at the bottom of the toy box, along with Raggedy Ann and Andy and the jack-in-the-box toy I wished someone would throw out. It took a few nights to feel safe enough to sleep with that killer doll in my room. When my mother noticed I shoved it at the bottom, she didn't even have to ask why. She already thought about how much the doll looked like Chucky. When my father noticed I hid My Buddy, I got in trouble for making him waste his money. He told me I better start playing with the stupid fucking doll or else. I didn't know what "else" was or did I want to find out. I took the toy out and played in front of my father to please him while thinking about how he wasted his own money because I told him I did not want that doll.

Anytime we visited my grandma, OJ would bitch at me, saying he knew I was not practicing. Anja wasn't as mean about it as she was becoming nicer to me for some reason. I wasn't sure why, but I liked the new and improved Anja. She was starting to defend me when OJ would hurt me or if he was too much to handle and would make me cry. I loved hearing her tell him off.

One night when my father needed to go somewhere without us while our mother was at work, he brought us to Grandma's, and Greta agreed to let us stay. I learned why Anja had been kind to me. While we all had to do sex stuff, there was something Anja expected me to do and do well. She laid on her back on her bed and told me I had to go down on her until she said she was coming. I had no clue what any of that meant. OJ and Anja explained it to me. OJ called me stupid for not knowing what eating someone out meant.

When I got closer to Anja's private area, I wanted to puke. I never smelled something so awful and tried to pull away. Anja wrapped her legs around me to keep me where she wanted me. I kept bitching that it was smelly and tasted so nasty, and I tried to wriggle myself free when Anja put both of her hands on the back of my head, forcing me into position. I didn't have a choice but to do what she said. I kept gagging, but she did not care. All of a sudden, Anja whisper-yelled, "I'm coming!" She freed me, and I jumped backward away from her, telling her how disgusting that was and how I would never do that again. Luckily for me, she didn't want me to anyway. My buck teeth kept scratching her, and she preferred someone who didn't have such big, sharp teeth. It didn't even hurt my feelings that I was now getting teased, and I didn't mind them reciting lines from Looney Tunes.

I was proud of my big, sharp teeth since they got me out of ever having to taste a nasty vagina again. OJ noticed me gloating and reminded me I still have to do other sex stuff when they tell me to. He said he could tell I was not practicing on My Buddy and that I better start practicing; he was tired of explaining everything to me more than once or twice. OJ informed me that he would also have little Jakob teach me while he's around me and OJ's not. He said, "The more you practice, the faster you will learn."

I didn't understand why OJ could not grasp that I did not want to learn, yet he thought I was stupid.

The next few times my mother took me to Aunt Alana's house, little Jakob and I would practice. He knew how to do sex stuff, but I had a feeling he didn't want to be doing it just as I didn't. I told him we didn't have to listen to OJ. I shared how I haven't practiced on My Buddy even though OJ told me I had to. Little Jakob put a scared look on his face and told me we had to do what OJ said and that he was the boss of everything. I didn't understand why little Jakob was afraid of OJ. OJ had Jakob in height, but while OJ was a skinny kid, little Jakob was husky. Everyone could tell he would grow big like his father and older brother, Raymond. But still, little Jakob complained that he was tired of OJ beating him up, so now he does everything OJ tells him to.

We would practice in the main closet, and one day, Raymond and my sister thought we were playing hide-and-seek, and while searching, they caught us. They agreed not to tell on us, but Raymond did make us get out of the closet. Another time, Aunt Alana was the one who caught us. She was pretty upset and yelled at both of us to pull our pants back up and get the fuck out of the closet. Before we could finish buttoning our pants back up, my mother came storming over to see what I was up to that upset her sister. Once she saw, her eyes grew wide behind her thick eyeglass lenses. When my mother was angry, one eye moved quickly from left to right while the other eye stayed looking straight at you. It reminded me of Cruella de Vil from *101 Dalmatians*. Seeing this made me know my mother was going to be demanding answers.

I didn't want to have to talk about what had just happened. I hated myself for doing it because it made me feel like a freak of nature. I knew talking about it would make me feel worse. My mother brought me to the living room so we could talk, and she began by saying that sex was for adults and not for blood-related people. My mother was sure she knew where I learned it and pointed out that she corrected my aunt Greta when she said kissing cousins was normal and that all children experiment. She said she always tells her sister, "No, it's not normal and not all children do it." My mother said she would like to be able to say, "Not my children."

I told her I was sorry and I would never do it again. We went back inside, and I apologized to my aunt. Little Jakob and I had to play either where our mothers could see us or our siblings could. We could hear our mothers agree that this was Greta and Otto's fault for not raising their kids right. We agreed with them, and once they noticed we were in their conversation, they yelled at us to mind our business and told us to go by our siblings. We laughed together as we joined Ada and Raymond in the bedroom. We loved bugging our mothers, they both had similar reactions like twins, and I loved it even more when my cousin reenacted his parents yelling at him. Even more, I loved that we didn't do sex stuff again for the rest of the visit. Our mothers awkwardly brought it up again before we left, saying they were glad our fathers weren't around because we'd both get our asses beat.

OJ was pleased to learn that little Jakob was doing what he told him to. Little Jakob assured him that I practiced, but OJ was unsure if he was telling the truth, knowing how I acted at his house while he and Anja were trying to teach me. OJ did not care that we had gotten caught by our mothers. He told us we had to keep doing it until he felt I no longer needed practice and to try harder not to get caught.

After a few times of not getting caught, we snuck off to the closet, and our mothers noticed they couldn't see or hear us and grew suspicious. My mother immediately checked the closet where my aunt had caught us last time and found her nephew lying on top of her daughter. She couldn't help but scream at us louder than her sister had when she caught us. Aunt Alana was right behind her and yelled at us some more. My mother took me into the backyard to talk this time. I felt like disappearing because she was talking to me as if she thought it was what I wanted to do. She explained that if blood-related people have sex, they could go to jail, and she told me that if a woman got pregnant by a blood relative, their baby could come out deformed. I asked what deformed meant, and she told me the baby could be missing an arm, its head too big or too small, and the baby might even come out looking like an alien. An image of me having given birth to an alien baby popped into my head, and then another one of the infant getting handed to its father, OJ. I was so afraid that would happen to me. I just knew that OJ would be the one to get me pregnant, and then the world would hate me.

As my mother continued the talk, I interrupted her by telling her that OJ was making little Jakob and me do sex stuff and that we didn't want to. She said that OJ was not our boss and we didn't ever have to do a damn thing he said. She also said I couldn't blame

OJ since he wasn't there. Little Jakob and I had to accept the blame for our actions and not place it on someone else. But my mother informed me that she was aware OJ was most likely where we learned the shit from since his father left porno movies out in the open, not caring if his kids pop the tape in the VCR and watch it themselves. I figured it would be wise to tell my mother that Uncle Otto does that on purpose and that OJ told me he lets them watch it. My mother knew her brother-in-law was a dirty, perverted pig but doubted that he would allow his children to watch the shit, so my mom told me OJ was lying to me about that. She told me that to prove it, she would bring it up to her sister, Greta.

I regretted telling my mother too much. Now OJ would find out I tattled. He would probably beat me up for it too. The next time I saw him, OJ bitched me out for it and threatened if I ever told on him again, my cousins would get my father to beat my ass. I was shocked when OJ didn't even punch my arm. I just had to listen and do sex stuff with him and Anja. And this time, I had to give OJ a blow job.

CHAPTER 31

Not *La Bamba*, You Cry Too Much

While my mother had decided I could handle watching *Bambi* without going into hysterics, she would put it on for me when I'd ask her to. But now there was a different movie I loved so much, *La Bamba*, and it would tear my mother apart seeing me crying so hard as soon as you'd hear the mother screaming "Not my Ritchy!" as her son had just died in a plane crash. She didn't know I started crying before that scene because I knew what was coming, and I had imagined the actress and actor was my aunt Alana and her son, Raymond. I didn't know why, but my father was mad at me, telling me I had to keep my mouth shut and not speak of anything to a soul. He accused me of trying to screw up everyone's plan to make America great again. I thought to myself, *What the heck is Daddy talking about? Tell who what? And when the fuck was America ever great?* I knew not to ask questions, especially during his ranting and raving, and he never specified who I supposedly told what to, so I remained oblivious to why he was scolding me. I was used to getting in trouble for nothing and assumed he was in one of his bad moods again.

I was trying to watch my favorite movie, *La Bamba*, when my father decided to be a pain in my ass. I figured I could pretend I was listening and instead keep listening to the television. I was good at tuning my father out and tuning in something that interested me. My father was also good at catching me, and he bitched more about me daydreaming and asked if I wanted to die out in the world from not paying attention to him when he was trying to teach me a lesson. He then bitched that I was watching that movie with wetbacks in it and who cared that her son died since that would be one less immigrant in the world. He grunted and said how he wished it were real, and he could see I was getting irritated with him not letting me watch.

My father watched, and once that sad scene started, he told me that since my favorite cousin was Raymond, the next time I opened my mouth, that would be my aunt screaming for her son because he would die a horrible sudden death. He teased my cousin, saying he was a nobody so his death wouldn't get revealed publicly as a celebrity would, and I'd be lucky if he let me go to his funeral. So now, anytime I'd ask my mother to watch *La Bamba*, she'd say, "Not *La Bamba*, pick something else." I'd beg her, and she'd say, "No, it makes you cry too much like you did with *Bambi*, and it breaks my heart seeing you so hysterical."

During the next visit to my aunt Alana's, I got emotional with Raymond and gave him the tightest, longest hug. While hugging me back with just as much love, he asked, "What's this for?"

I released him so I could look straight into his eyes and said, "Because you are my favorite cousin."

He hugged me again and kissed my forehead, joking that I had my father's forehead. I joked and said, "I know, I hate my big forehead."

Raymond assured me I looked cute with the size of my forehead, and we joked that my father looked silly with his large shiny forehead. Little Jakob was getting mad at me because he wanted to play outside in the backyard, far enough so as not to be seen. I knew why, and I didn't feel like having to practice to please our cousins, Anja and OJ. I didn't want to do it the first time or any time. More so now since I couldn't shake off the feeling that I would lose my favorite cousin, Raymond. It was already hard enough fighting the tears from falling, and little Jakob was making it more difficult with his constant bugging.

I ran into the kitchen by our mothers and hid under the table, sneaking up every few minutes to steal sips of my mother's coffee so we could leave. I had to leave that house because I felt very anxious and like my heart was about to explode. My mother ran to the bathroom, and my aunt went to make herself another cup of coffee, so I hopped up and took a big sip of my mother's coffee.

As they both were seated again, my mother called out, "Ilse Leigh, I know you drank my coffee again. I'll just make another cup, thank you."

Little Jakob walked inside the kitchen and pointed out I was hiding under the table. My mother said she knew and got up to pour herself another cup, telling me to go inside and leave her coffee alone. I told my mother I was tired and didn't feel good, hoping Mommy would say we could leave, but instead, she told me to lie on the couch until she finished drinking her coffee. She promised to drink it fast. She did drink it faster than usual, but not fast enough to prevent little Jakob from following me and bugging me some more, telling me he knew I was feeling fine and he didn't want OJ to beat him up for not making me practice.

I told him I was feeling too sick, and OJ wouldn't beat him up for me being sick. He called me a liar and finally let me be until it was time to say goodbye. I loved my cousin dearly as he was another one of my favorites, but I was glad to be leaving because he was making me feel like I wished I was never born. Back at home, I started wondering if life would have been better for me if I had been born a boy like the doctors said I would be.

CHAPTER 32

I'm Adam Wilheim

When a short while ago we had gotten new neighbors in the house where Imani used to live, I noticed there was a white family, a mom, a dad, and two daughters. One daughter looked about my age, and the other was maybe two years younger. I thought it was pretty cool because that was exactly how our house was. I wanted to become friends with the girl who looked to be my age, but I was only going to introduce myself to her as my outside self, Ilse Leigh. I could not let her find out that I was a boy named Adam Wilheim when inside the house.

Since little Jakob made me wish I was a boy, I had started trying to turn myself into one. I was getting excited because as soon as I could be a full boy, little Jakob and I would fuck OJ up. I didn't know how I would change into a boy, and I had already told my mother that I wanted to be a boy instead of a girl, but she replied, "Sorry, you're stuck with the way you were born." I thought that maybe my mother didn't know how to change from a girl to a boy or she liked having two girls so she didn't want to tell me.

Anytime I was alone in the bathroom, I began pulling on the two flappy pieces of skin on my vagina, stretching them as far as they would go. While I thought my vagina would change into a penis, it only became soar and red, and it hurt when I wiped after using the toilet. That didn't stop me from trying to accomplish my goal though. I still did it until one day my mother walked into the bathroom and caught me, screaming as if she had seen a mouse in the house, "Oh my god, Ilse Leigh, stop that! What the hell are you trying to do?"

Embarrassed, I looked up at my mother and said, "I want to be Adam Wilheim. I don't want to be stupid Ilse Leigh anymore."

Feeling bad that she hadn't explained it more to me than just saying I was stuck with the way I was born, my mother decided it was time to explain that I wouldn't be able to change myself into a boy, and she told me that I should love myself for who I am. I reminded her that some of my cousins act like boys, especially Chrissy. My mother chuckled and taught me the meaning of the word tomboy. She said it was when a girl sometimes pretended to be a boy, doing boyish things or even dressing like a boy. I told her Chrissy did all those things, and she even sounded like a boy.

I asked, "Mommy, can I be a tomboy like Chrissy?"

I was ecstatic when she said yes. I practiced talking like a boy, repeating the introduction of my tomboy self, "Hi, I'm Adam Wilheim."

One day, while my sister wouldn't play with me and my mother was too busy on the phone, I was getting so irritable and didn't know what to do with myself, so I stripped down to my underwear and began running around like a crazy monkey. When running into the living room, I'd jump on one side of the couch and run to the other, step up on the arm of the couch, and jump off to continue running. My sister kept yelling at me to put some clothes on, saying that was disgusting, and she ran to tell our mother. I heard my mother tell the person on the other line of the phone to hold on, and then she asked me what I was doing, parading around in just my underwear. I jumped on one end of the couch, ran to the other, stood on the arm of the chair, and as I jumped off, I yelled in a boyish tone, "I'm Adam Wilheim!"

She asked me not to jump on the furniture and to please put some clothes on. I told my mother that OJ ran around in his underwear at Grandma's house. Remembering that I was now a tomboy, my mother told my sister that it was okay for me to want to be a tomboy and to ignore the fact that I was naked. Then she told me that I had to make sure never to do that in front of my father and I was to have clothes on before he got home. I said okay and ran freely, then my sister said, "Now I'm really not playing with you, you're so gross."

She ran into our room so she didn't have to look at me. When I finally put my clothes back on, my sister tried to convince me that girls do not run around in their underwear. We ended up in an argument since she couldn't get me to listen to her and I couldn't get her to understand that I wanted to be a tomboy and Mommy said I was allowed.

We both got yelled at for arguing, but my mother looked at my sister and said, "And you, stop trying to be her mother hen, I'm her mother, and I told her she can run around naked when your father's not home."

After my mother left the room, my sister told me she was not looking forward to seeing me naked all summer and that I better hurry up and stop wanting to be a tomboy.

Every time I saw my new neighbor, I admired her. She had long, beautiful, dark-brown hair. I can remember when I had long hair before I accidentally pulled a coffeepot over me and got burned. I was so mad at myself for that. And now my father wouldn't even let my hair grow much past my shoulders. As soon as he felt it was too long, I'd have to get it cut. I loved when I had long hair because, in the sunlight, my hair looked golden and reminded me of Rapunzel. For some reason, my father hated it. When I would point it out to him, he would yell at me and say my hair was brown. I didn't say it wasn't brown, so he confused me, but my father had a habit of not making any sense. I guessed he would be happy once I was a boy instead of a girl since he liked making me look like one. And he did buy me a boy doll, so maybe it was what he wanted anyway.

As I watched my neighbor ride her bike, her long, beautiful hair blowing in the wind, I wondered if someday we would become boyfriend and girlfriend. I was still a girl, so I didn't like girls, only boys. I also thought about how glad I was that I quickly learned to ride my Strawberry Shortcake bike because my neighbor knew how to ride one. I was so embarrassed while my mother and sister would teach me, and I would pray the neighbor wouldn't come outside and see me.

One summer day, while my mother brought my sister and me out to play, the neighbor was also out with her mom and sister. I asked my mother if we could say hi by the gate that separated our yards as we did with Imani and her mom. My mother was hesitant at first because she didn't want me to make another friend that I wasn't going to be allowed to play with, knowing that my father claimed the house itself was a filthy welfare house. I told my mother it would probably be okay since the new neighbors were white. She figured I was probably right, and we introduced ourselves.

The girl my age was named Adessa. Her younger sister was Vikki. Vikki was such a cute little girl. She loved to carry around her favorite toy, and if she'd trip or bump into something, not paying attention to where she was walking, she'd yell out, "Ouchie." She had short hair like me, but hers was pin-straight while my hair was straight at the roots and wavy farther down and the bottom was curly.

Adessa became my best friend faster than we could learn each other's names. She didn't live with her father. Adessa had a stepfather. As my mother felt the need to apologize beforehand for her husband's strict ways, she told the mother that we would have to make sure my father would be okay with us being friends and hanging out. Adessa's mother was familiar with strict parenting and said her husband was the same way. I had to wait for my father to be in a good mood to ask if I could be friends with Adessa.

When I asked him, he bitched because they were clearly on welfare if they lived in a welfare house. I didn't see what made it a welfare house since it was about the same size as ours. I gave my father my sad kitty face and said, "I thought it would be okay since they are white."

To my surprise, my father couldn't say no to his precious Kitten Lee, and I was officially best friends with my new neighbor, Adessa.

My sister was relieved that becoming friends with Adessa made me realize I liked being a girl. I no longer wished to become Adam Wilheim. I told her it was a stupid name anyway. My sister admitted to me that she didn't mind when I made myself sound like a boy since that was funny, but she could not deal with me ripping off my clothes and running around naked the moment I was sure my father was off to work and wouldn't be back for hours. But now, instead of that, I was eagerly waiting for it to be time for my mother to take us outside to play.

Adessa was allowed to come over although my father had warned my mother that she better not let her inside the house. My mother ignored his wishes, and if we wanted to play inside the house, we could. We would have to clean up and get back outside before it was time for my father to come home. My sister got along with Adessa well, but there were a few things she didn't feel comfortable with. Adessa liked to act like a sexy woman a lot, and she sometimes talked about sex stuff. My sister would ask her to stop, and Adessa would respect her wishes as I would think of what we could do instead.

If my sister was no longer around us, Adessa would start acting like a sexy woman again. We never really got to hang out on weekends since that was when Adessa would go have visitation with her father. I missed her while she was gone, but it worked out because it wasn't long before my father kept threatening that he would stop us from being friends, calling Adessa a slut.

At first, I was furious at my sister, thinking she spoke to our father about Adessa's occasional inappropriate behavior. When I confronted her, she assured me that if she had told our father, I would no longer be allowed to hang out with Adessa. My sister hadn't even told my mother, but she said she didn't care if Adessa wanted to act that way at her house. She was not going to allow her to behave that way at ours. I agreed that was fair and apologized to my sister for accusing her of doing something she didn't. While during my father's rants and calling my best friend a slut, I would keep my mouth shut as I was screaming at my father in my head.

When my mother would hear him, she would defend Adessa and say, "Don't call Ilse's friend a slut, she's just a little girl. How can she be a slut?"

My father would talk under his breath, or he would tell her she didn't know what the fuck she was talking about and he'd say that girl was a slut. If the argument continued, he'd call my mother a slut, and then I'd have to hear him make her have sex that night.

CHAPTER 33

Anja Doesn't Do Sex Stuff Anymore

My father had left my mother with no choice but to quit her job, arguing that she needed to be home with their kids. It was becoming an issue also with our aunt Greta constantly bitching at our mother for having to watch us longer than she was supposed to because our father would say he had important shit he had to take care of. My mother was so devastated that she had to quit her job. I would hear her tell someone over the phone that she misses her time away from the house and how she felt good bringing in money that my father couldn't tell her how to spend. Now it was back to living off scraps of change and collecting bottles and cans again.

One night, while visiting my grandma's, Aunt Greta demanded all the kids go upstairs to Anja and OJ's room. OJ popped a porno in the VCR after telling us that after watching a little bit, we would have to do what the people on TV were doing. I was sitting on Anja's bed near her and my sister while little Jakob and OJ were sitting on the floor in front of the TV. Usually, when my mother was ready to go soon, she would open the door at the bottom of the stairs and yell loud enough for us to hear her call us with the door at the top of the stairs closed. This night, my mother decided to come up and get us.

Anja and my sister heard the bottom door open, and someone began walking up the stairs. They held hands, jumped off the bed, and ran into her parents' bedroom, pretending to have been playing with the kitchen set she hadn't played with in ages.

Then I heard my mother say, "C'mon, girls, it's time to get ready to go."

Her voice got louder as she opened the second door, and I didn't know what else to do but cover my eyes as I cried out, "I didn't want to watch it, Mommy, OJ made me."

Too zoned into the TV, little Jakob and OJ had no clue of their surroundings until my mother yelled, "Uh, excuse me! Turn this fucking shit off right now and give it to me."

My mother brought her daughters and the porno downstairs and handed it to her sister. "Greta, tell your husband to stop leaving his damn porn movies out for OJ to get ahold of."

She had informed her that my sister and Anja were being good, playing in the other room, but I was in the kids' room when OJ put it on. All my aunt had to say of the matter was, "Oh gee, yeah Big Otto's always forgetting to put those away."

I was happy that my mother didn't think I wanted to be watching porn, but I felt abandoned by my sister. It was one thing that Anja didn't grab my hand and save me from getting in trouble, but I never thought my sister, my savior, would leave me for dead. It was nothing like when we were in our backyard, playing where she was my hero and saved me from my evil father who kept me locked away in his tower. It felt like my hero fed me to the wolves chasing us from outside. The one who was my savior was only concerned with saving herself. Later, when we went home, she acted like nothing was wrong, so I did too. I knew she wouldn't let me talk about it anyway since she never spoke of it unless it was happening at that moment.

After that night, the next few times I had to do sex stuff, it was only with OJ. Anja didn't have to do sex stuff anymore. I wasn't surprised that she didn't save me. And most times, she would take my sister to another area of the house to play, and I had to play with OJ, either up in his room or sometimes in the basement if the room was where Ada and Anja were playing. My sister only had to do sex stuff with OJ when Anja wasn't home. I wasn't even mad at Anja or my sister for it.

Aunt Greta would say, "Let the girls go play to themselves, Ilse. They're older than you guys."

It was as if she thought I was one of the boys. I tried telling my aunt that I wasn't a tomboy anymore and that Anja and OJ were the same age, so nothing she said made sense to me, but my mother heard the way I was speaking to her sister with such attitude, and she yelled at me for disrespecting my aunt. So from that day on, I just did what I had to and cursed at Greta and OJ in my head on the way, during, and after.

When my aunt Eleven and uncle Jerry came out, their daughter, Catrina, no longer had to do sex stuff with OJ either. She got to go with Anja and do girl stuff. And so did Sasha when she'd come over, but like my sister, if Anja weren't around, Sasha would have to go not be seen or heard with OJ. My sister's boobs were beginning to grow, and I could see the shame and discomfort in her eyes as OJ would talk about how he loved her tits. I saw the same look in my aunt Heidi's eyes that summer.

As Aunt Eleven and Uncle Jerry were visiting one day, everyone was outside, and I ran into the house to use the bathroom. Aunt Heidi had been in her room sitting on her bed while my cousin, JJ was sucking on her boob. I didn't know what else to do, so I pretended not to see anything and went to the bathroom. When I finished and left the bathroom, JJ was sitting on the bed next to our aunt, acting as if nothing happened.

He called out to me and said, "Hey, Lee Lee, come here."

I just kept moving faster. I heard him say, "She's so cute." I ran out of the house and didn't look back. It wasn't hard to act like I saw nothing since I learned how to do that well from every person in my family. But it hurt not having anyone I could talk to about things that happened in my family.

As I always dreaded the moment I would begin attending the district of evil racists, I also could not wait so I wouldn't have to be around my family as much. I felt like I was becoming dizzy, and sometimes I thought my body would explode. My head was constantly spinning images from behind my eyes. I could see constant clear visions of things that happened in my past. I knew I would be going to an evil school of racism, but at least I wouldn't have to see people fighting or doing sex stuff, and I knew no one would be hitting me or making me do sex stuff.

It wasn't long after my female cousins stopped doing sexual things with us that my sister put her foot down. One day, while visiting our grandma's house, Aunt Greta repeated her usual command directed toward OJ, my sister, and me. OJ loved that my sister's boobs, or as he always called them tits or titties, had seemed to get bigger every time he saw them. I could tell that it bothered my sister as her face cringed slightly every time he said those words. I hated hearing those words too. Or that he called a vagina a pussy. I felt like I was going to puke in my mouth at the sound of it, especially since what I had to do to Anja before she stopped doing sex stuff.

As my sister sat on the floor, it was as if you could read the words shame and sorrow on her face while OJ was molesting her growing chest with his mouth and hands. She pulled away, saying, "I can't anymore, I feel so sick, I have to go downstairs."

No sooner than she said it, she was heading downstairs without me again. And no faster than she left did OJ then continue to molest me. He made fun of me for not having any titties for him to play with and lick as he did so. I wanted to run downstairs, but I had a feeling for a while now that my aunt or somebody was telling my father that I wasn't behaving or something since every time I didn't listen to my aunt when she told me to play and not be seen or heard or if I'd tell OJ no to sex stuff, I'd get a beating for I didn't know what because my father never made sense to me.

It sucked when I was coming up with a cold and told my aunt no because I didn't feel well and needed to lie down. My grandmother would let me lay in her bed until I felt good enough to get back up or until I was leaving to go home. My father would then give me a beating, claiming I did something I didn't, and my mother would have to yell at him to stop because I wasn't feeling good. If I had a fever, my mother would say, "Feel her head." He would feel it and swear I was burning up, and he would baby me, apologizing for beating me when I learned a long time ago that he was never sorry; otherwise, he wouldn't do it again.

I was happy still, with my father now making me comfortable, putting on a movie I wanted to watch, and he would let me watch it for once instead of distracting me during the good scenes as he would also make sure I was concentrating on the bad ones.

CHAPTER 34

The Birds and the Bees

My father had been especially cranky with my sister. He was pissing me off more and more each time, calling her a fat lard of shit. He was also bitching at my mother when she dared to ask him to waste his money on a new bed that would fit my sister and me. The first time she asked, my father told her if she had not quit her job, we could afford to buy a new bed. My mother reminded him that he was the reason she had to stop working since he didn't want to watch the kids he helped her make. He said that only one of the girls was his, Ilse. As he always did when angry, he accused my sister of being his brother Heinrich's daughter.

The next time Ada and I were home alone with our father, we were in the living room when our father came in and told my sister to go to his bedroom so they could talk about the birds and bees. I thought *Wow, Daddy's finally in a good mood, and he's going to tell us a story about birds and bees* as I followed them to the bedroom. My father hadn't even realized I was in the room until he shut the door and turned around and saw me.

I was smiling at him, waiting for him to begin the story, but instead, he yelled, "What the fuck are you doing here? I didn't tell you to come with us."

I was confused and thought maybe he was joking. I didn't see why he wouldn't want me to join. I told him I wanted to hear about birds, and before I could say bees, my father yelled, "Uh, stupid, not that kind of birds and bees. You're too young to hear about sex, so get the fuck in the living room."

As I walked out of the room, I wondered why he didn't just call it the "bad thing" or sex like he usually did instead of calling it birds and bees. My father then told me I was to keep the volume loud on the TV so I don't listen in on their conversation and I couldn't sit on the couch. I had to sit on his chair. I nodded my head, yes, assuming he wouldn't hear me if I said the word anyway. At least if he had been watching me leave, as I had a strong sense he was, then my father would see I agreed to obey.

Once I was in the living room and turned the volume up a few notches, I could hear my sister cry and scream, so I assumed our father was disciplining her, and then he yelled, "Stop crying, or I'll give you something to cry for."

Knowing he was beating her, I started to cry. It wasn't long before they came out of the room. I stopped crying and wiped my tears. My father joined me in the living room, and my sister went straight to our bedroom. I was glad he stopped hurting my sister. I didn't want him near me, but I had a bad feeling that I should stay put. I looked at my father with a concerned look and asked, "Do you want your chair, Daddy?"

He said, "Yeah."

So I went over and sat on the couch.

He asked, "What shit are you watching?" He then grabbed the remote to change the channel. He didn't tell me I could go to my room, so I waited until my mother returned home.

She came in, saying she had to pee, and I thought, *Yeah, me too. Thank God you're home. I was afraid to move.*

Later, when I felt it was a better time to try and cheer my sister up over getting a beating for nothing, she didn't feel like talking. I had a lot of time to think since I sat on the couch bored for a while and thought of a plan to try and convince my father to get us a new bed. When I told my sister the idea, she told me not to ask him for anything for her. I pleaded with her to see that she deserved it as much as I did.

My sister said, "No, I don't want anything from him. He can buy you a new bed, and I'll sleep on this one. Then if I get too fat for it, I'll sleep on the floor."

Knowing my sister needed more time to herself, I softly said, "I'm sorry Daddy hurt you, I love you."

When my mother asked what was wrong, she said she was tired.

*****

OJ was getting on my case a lot about me not knowing how to do what he told me to, accusing me of pretending not to know how to do it right. He said I better start practicing on My Buddy or he would have my father give me the worst beating of my life. I told him it wasn't fair that Anja or my sister or any of the female cousins for that matter didn't have to do sex stuff anymore. I pointed out to him that he never gets my father to beat my sister, only me. OJ said it was because my father abused her enough while claiming that my father doesn't beat me enough. He also stated that the girls in the family were older than me, so they had other things to do. Realizing that if I didn't listen to OJ, I would be facing my father beating me worse than he ever had.

I started to practice with My Buddy but only when I knew I had alone time in my bedroom. I hated doing it, and as I did, I allowed myself to escape and find my brain's safe spot enough to where I wouldn't get lost and could still hear if someone was coming near my room. In case, I surrounded myself with other toys and kept myself fully dressed so I wouldn't get caught. I felt disgusting inside but was glad that I was the one who said when the practice began and ended. It was beyond awkward being around my family after the fact but knowing they had no clue it happened helped me feel better about being a nasty freak of nature.

As my sister had been so sad for a while, it was nice seeing her laugh when I called myself a freak of nature and a human bean. When she heard that I said "bean" instead of being, she taught me the correct way of pronouncing human beings. Thanking her for always teaching me things I need to know in life, I said, "I know, sissy, but I'm not a human being, I'm a freak of nature, I'm a freaking human bean." We both couldn't stop laughing, and I couldn't have been happier to see my sister happy again. Even better was when we finally played together again.

The schools would be opening soon as Adessa and I waited impatiently for the letter to come and we would see what teacher we would have. We were hoping we could be in the same class and agreed we'd feel better being around each other in a new place with new people. I thought about how nice it would be to hang out with Adessa and not hear my sister be so mean to her. She said she was tired of my friend being disrespectful as my sister had to keep sounding like a broken record, "Adessa, stop acting all sexy. Adessa, stop talking about sex." She claimed to have had enough and told Adessa if she didn't stop it, she would tell our mother and then she wouldn't be allowed over anymore.

I was upset because I couldn't control my friend, who kept lifting her shirt and rubbing her body when my sister blew up at her. I didn't want to lose my friend, but I also didn't want my sister to think I was picking Adessa's side when we finally got back to saying good night in the special way we learned from *The Aristocats*. Not being the type who chooses sides, I made Adessa play outside with me as I spoke to her about respecting my sister's wishes. I asked her why she did that stuff anyway, and she said she did it because she liked it. Knowing that I learned that kind of stuff from my cousins, I asked Adessa who taught it to her. I was worried about my best friend.

She said, "The TV."

I asked her who showed it to her on TV, and she replied, "Nobody, I found it."

I had a feeling that Adessa's cousins might be molesting her, and I hoped that she would tell me so I could get her help. I didn't tell her that I had to do sex stuff with my cousins because I didn't know if she would call me a freak and never speak to me anymore. Plus, I couldn't risk her trying to save me, then my father would find out, and he would give me the worst beating ever. Not to mention, it was awkward enough being around everyone that didn't know about kids having incest orgy sessions, so telling someone could blow it up, and I knew it would only be more awkward if they knew.

One thing I disliked about my family was that when you told someone something, it only took an hour for the whole family, plus friends of the family, to have already heard about it. It made me feel sick to think about it, so I told Adessa I was tired and wanted to go inside and nap. After she left, I went inside and apologized to my sister for my friend's behavior. She complained that it was disrespectful for Adessa to keep doing it, and my sister was tired of telling her. I told her I understood and that I had a talk with Adessa about it. I shared my idea of trying not to play in the same room my sister was in but kindly asked my sister if she could be nicer to Adessa when she was around.

She got loud and said, "I tried being nice for a while!"

I got nervous and moved closer to my sister to whisper, "Shhh, Mommy's not deaf. She'll hear you."

My sister smiled and softly spoke, "Ma-ma, ma-ma." Then she yelled, "Mom!"

Unsure if she was going to tell, I got scared once our mother called out, "What?"

My sister spoke loud enough for my mother to hear, "I wasn't calling you."

I was able to release my breath. We were both laughing, and I said I wanted to try it. Doing exactly what my sister had, our mother yelled, "What do you want?"

We laughed loudly, and I yelled, "Nothing, I wasn't calling you."

Then it was my sister's turn again, and our mother did not like the game we were playing as she yelled, "What do you girls want? I'm trying to finish cooking before your father gets home, or we'll hear his mouth."

My sister yelled, "We'll stop now. We were joking."

That night, we played a game before bed since our father made us go to bed early so he could watch porn in the living room before lying down with his wife. It was the same as earlier, but this time, we would say, "Da-da, da-da...Dad." And we had to be somewhat loud while trying not to be the one he heard.

When he heard, he yelled, "Girls, go to bed, or I'll come in there."

We knew damn well he was not taking his eyes off his disgusting porn, but we didn't continue the game.

My sister said, "See ya in the morning, Napoleon."

I responded, "Good night, Lafayette."

Then when our mother came in to say good night, and we went to sleep.

CHAPTER 35

Ms. Mato, Like Tomato

The school letters arrived, and I learned that Adessa did not have the same teacher as me. I was nervous, so my mother tried convincing me there was no reason to be afraid and that school was fun. She told me that at least I could still see Adessa at the bus stop and on the bus to and from school. Then she reminded me that we were neighbors anyway.

I explained to my mother that unlike my sister, who had been going to school before kindergarten, this was my first time, and it was scary knowing that my sister or mother wouldn't be there to protect me. My mother said the teacher would help me if I needed her to. It wasn't enough, but I smiled and said, "Okay, Mommy."

It was time to go school shopping, and our father had to spend money on school clothes, so he bitched as he handed our mother money to take us shopping and barked, "Only two outfits and one pair of sneakers each."

My mother said we would need dress shoes and sneakers, and he was angry until she said she didn't need any more money. With a small amount of money, my mother managed to buy my sister and me each three outfits, a pair of sneakers, and dress shoes. We also got new undies and socks, and my sister had to get training bras to cover her growing boobs.

When we got home, my father bitched that we had more than two outfits each and that he never told my mother she could buy us socks and underwear and stuff. He complained to her that she was supposed to bring him back the change. I knew where he got that from, his father before him. My father always told me the story about how, one time, my grandfather gave my grandmother two dollars to go food shopping. When she came home with the groceries and no change left over, my grandfather yelled at her, "You spent the whole two dollars?"

As we put our stuff away, my mother let us try our clothes on one more time, and when I put on my dress shoes, I asked my mother why it was called dress shoes. She said there were all kinds of names for fancy shoes, so I asked if I could call them "bang" shoes since they made banging sounds when I danced around in them and tapped them as Dorothy did with her ruby red slippers. My shoes weren't red; they were black with a pretty black bow. When I showed my father, he yelled at me for wearing my new stuff and said not to touch it again until school started. I thought about how I couldn't wait for that day to come. Everything was ready, school supplies and clothes shopping were complete, our hair got trimmed, and we had to wait for the first day of school.

The night before school reopened, I had a hard time getting to sleep, thinking about all the things I did that summer. I started feeling empty inside once the thought of me leaving my mother for half of the day appeared. She had been saying she couldn't wait until I went to school so she could have some quiet for once. I knew she didn't mean it though. My mother loved being around her daughters, and when she wasn't around, she missed the heck out of us.

It seemed like I had finally fallen asleep when I woke up in the morning. It was still dark out, so I knew I had time, and I just laid in bed thinking. I felt sick and thought my mother would have to keep me home. I told her I felt ill, but she told me it was my nerves and that I had nothing to be nervous about. The more I hung out with my mother, the less jittery I felt.

When my sister woke up, we ate breakfast and put our new stuff on for school. First, we had to walk my sister to her bus stop. After her bus picked her up, we went home for a few minutes until it was time to go to my bus stop. A girl who dressed like a snobby rich kid was there. I said hi after she did but was in no mood for an introduction, so I stayed close to my mother. When Adessa arrived, she said hi to me and started talking to the other girl.

The bus came, so my mother said goodbye to me and said, "Now don't cry, okay? You'll be okay, I promise. I'll know if you cry, too, because when you cry, it makes me cry."

I promised not to cry. My mommy hugged and kissed me goodbye, and I got on the bus, being as brave as I could. It was hard to keep the tears from falling, watching my mother wave to me from the window. I waited until she couldn't see me anymore, and the tears rolled down my face. I wished the bus would stop and let me off so I could run back into my mommy's arms and never leave her again.

In the classroom, there were so many cool toys and games. I still missed my mommy like hell, but I found comfort in knowing I would be having fun. The teacher seemed nice; she had us all sit on a rug in a circle and introduce ourselves. She started by saying she was Ms. Mato, like a tomato. That way, it would be easy to remember her name.

As each student thought of a word to match their name, I couldn't think of anything. My turn was up, and I blurted out "Igloo Ilse" and immediately told myself how stupid that was. After everyone finished, I asked Ms. Mato if I could change mine. She said the one I picked was a good choice and that we had to move on to the next thing she had planned. She could tell I was upset, so she asked the class who liked the name Igloo Ilse, and it seemed everyone did. Realizing that my teacher did that for me to make me happy, I knew it was going to be a great year. It also made me realize that my father didn't have as many eyes on me as he led me to believe, but just to be sure, I would still be careful.

When it was time for free play, I played with the kitchen stuff and saw a black baby doll. It reminded me of Imani, and I wanted to play with it but was afraid to. Although it was clear that my teacher was not spying on me, I didn't know about the students yet or the teacher's helper. I saw how everyone was distracted with other things and figured it was my chance to look at the beautiful black baby doll. As I went to pick it up, my classmate, Malerie, came over and snatched it before I could get it. I figured she may not have realized

I was going for it, so I kindly let her know I was about to play with that doll; thinking she would let me have it, she said no with an attitude and walked away. The white baby doll was not far from the black one, and I saw an image of me losing my best friend, Imani, all over again. I did not like that Malerie girl and knew she would be a problem this year.

Seeing that she didn't want to play with the doll in the first place as she put it down and went to play with something else, I ran over to grab the black baby doll and brought it back to the white baby doll. Once I could finally play, pretending the white one was me and the black one was Imani, Ms. Mato said the free play was over. I cursed Malerie out in my head and thought it didn't matter because I would have the doll to play with the whole school year, and I didn't care if she told my father because I would say that she was a liar. All I needed to do was make a sad kitty face, and my father would believe me over her for sure; she had dirty blonde hair.

Once it was time to get on the bus to leave, I was anxiously excited to return home to my mommy. I couldn't wait to tell her about my day at school and how much I loved going. When the bus got to my stop, there was my beautiful mother, the biggest smile and the glow in her eyes showing how much she missed me too. I ran to hug her and told her my day was great.

She said, "That's great. I missed you so much! And I know you cried this morning 'cause I cried too."

I smiled and told her I did. As Adessa and the other girl walked together in front of us with their mothers, the two girls turned to me, and Adessa introduced me to her friend, Lydia. I was kind and said hi but told them I missed my mother and stayed by her. While that was true, I also didn't trust that Lydia was a true friend. I noticed on the bus that she was very nosy and quite bossy to my friend, Adessa. Lydia had brown hair like me.

The more I went to school, the more I couldn't wait to learn. We learned about some historical people from the past, the Indians. Something I had wanted my entire life on Earth so far was to know about my Indian heritage. I thought of Bowie the whole lesson and thought about asking my father if he could please bring me to see

Bowie. While my teacher taught about Indians, I didn't know which Indian was my ancestor. Bowie didn't either, but he seemed to know about my heritage, and I just had to learn. Plus, I missed Bowie so much. My father always had to take the ones I loved who would be part of my army away from me. That or he made them want to move away from us, like Imani's family.

When I found the right time to ask my father, he smiled big and was amazed that I remembered Bowie. "How do you remember him, kit?"

Shrugging my shoulders, I said, "I don't know. I just do. So can we go see him at his hot dog truck?"

My father explained that Bowie's name was Barry, and we couldn't go to see him because the fucking n—— took over, so we did not go there anymore. He went on and on, and I was getting impatient waiting for the answer to my question and asked, "Can we see Bowie at our house?"

My father got so angry at me and told me I was stupid for not knowing Barry's name even though he told me over and over, and then he said, "Barry's gone."

The words rang in my ears, and I hoped for meaning to them, but my father didn't give me one or did I dare ask him to clarify. He bitched that I was too stupid to remember Barry's name, but I was smart by remembering him at all, complaining he would have to have more family gatherings. My father bitched because I was now turning six and was getting too old to sit on Daddy's lap to drink. I didn't understand what drinking had to do with remembering Bowie or that he told me I was allowed to call him Bowie every time my father corrected me. I wished my father would understand that I would never forget the people or places I loved so I wouldn't have to start drinking again. I was glad that he stopped making me do that. I didn't even go to Smitty's Pub anymore. I asked my father if we could do that instead of beer, and he said no because they couldn't risk getting caught distributing to minors, so I wasn't allowed in there anymore and not to worry because he had to wait until school was over anyway.

CHAPTER 36

A Fake Boyfriend to Trick Daddy

Since I got out of school earlier than my sister, I had plenty of time to play in my room with my door closed and practice having sex with My Buddy before it was time to leave for the bus stop. Anytime I did, I was so bored that I would get sleepy, and I always made sure I stopped practicing in time to catch a quick nap.

One day, I was so tired from the lack of sleep the night before since my father made my mother have sex again. I was going to say forget it and nap instead, but I kept hearing OJ in my head, bitching at me for not practicing every chance I got and he would get my father to beat my ass. I lay on the bed and pulled my pants down, putting My Buddy's face on my vagina so that he could eat it out. The next thing I knew, I woke up, and my mother stood over me, yelling at me to pull my pants up and questioning why I had my doll down there. I didn't know what to say, being I was embarrassed and still sleepy, so I told her I didn't know. She told me to hurry up and put my pants on so we could leave to get my sister. She reminded me to pee before we left the house and said we would talk later.

I didn't want to talk about it. I hoped to forget it, but I knew my mother would not let me. When she said we would talk about something later, we would, and then she would call my grandmother and a few of her sisters to tell them what happened. I wanted to die right then and there, but instead, I had to face the music. Being it was a situation where my mother didn't want to risk my father finding out, she would only tell the people she knew wouldn't tell him, so I was relieved that not the whole family would hear about it, but knowing that any of them knew made me feel so disgusted with myself.

My sister couldn't help herself but make me feel worse, telling me how disgusting I was and that I was not to ever put that doll near her or anything of hers, including our bed even though we shared it, because she didn't want my cooties touching her. My sister and our mother asked if I did that with any other toys, so I let them know it was only with My Buddy.

One Friday after school, Adessa came over to play, and we went into my room. I closed the door so we wouldn't bother my sister and mother with our loud mouths as I always did.

I heard my mother storming toward my room, and she swung the door open while saying, "You keep this bedroom door open from now on, Ilse Leigh."

I knew that was her rule when I went in there by myself so she didn't have to catch me humping my doll, but I wasn't aware that the rules still applied if I had company over. My mother made me so angry when Adessa asked what that was about. I told her my mother didn't trust me right now and she wanted me to keep my door open. Knowing that something was happening to Adessa, I thought about telling her the truth for a minute, but I decided it was best to leave it at that, especially since she didn't push the issue any further.

*****

There were twins on my bus that couldn't prevent me from realizing they had a crush on me. Their names were George and Geoffrey. They were Czechoslovakian and had blond hair. I wanted to date them both, but I knew someone like Malerie or Lydia would tell my father. I decided I would have to have a fake boyfriend so that I could tell my father that was my boyfriend. I wasn't allowed to have a boyfriend, so if my father did find out, I'd get in trouble anyway, but at least he would be happy that I was sticking with my own kind, which he claimed to be German.

During circle time, a boy, Kurt, sat next to me. He was cute, and he had brown hair and brown eyes. I didn't know if he was German, but he definitely was a white boy. Before I let any of these boys become my boyfriend, I would have to ask my mother if she was okay with it.

On the way home one day, George and Geoffrey were fighting over me because they both wanted to sit next to me, so the bus driver said one twin could sit by the window, I could sit in the middle, and the other twin could sit on the part of the seat closest to the aisle. Before I could get off at my stop, the bus driver had to tell my mother how cute it was that she had to give us our own seats or we wouldn't have left the school because the boys both had to sit next to me. My mother laughed and agreed it was cute as I was finally able to get off the bus. I was upset that I couldn't be the one to ask if I could have boyfriends, but I asked instead, "So I can have boyfriends?"

My mother laughed again and said it was okay with her because I was only in kindergarten, but once I got older, I would have to stick with only having one boyfriend at a time. I asked if she was okay with me having another boyfriend and the twins, and I told her about Kurt in school.

She said, "Okay, but that's it. No more boyfriends than the three."

I was so excited to tell George and Geoffrey on the bus the next day that they were allowed to be my boyfriends. I informed them that only my mother was okay with it and that I had to hide it from my father, so I would ask Kurt in my class to be my boyfriend but that he was only fake to trick my father. George didn't know Kurt because he wasn't in that class, but Geoffrey was, and he did know Kurt. They agreed because their father didn't like Germans, so they had to keep it a secret.

The plan to trick my father was working as Kurt said yes to being my boyfriend. I didn't mention the twins to him because I didn't want Kurt to say forget about being his girlfriend. That day, on the bus ride home, George asked if he and his brother could kiss me on my cheek goodbye. They were my boyfriends, so I didn't see my mother having a problem with it, and I let them kiss a cheek each before I got out of the seat.

A few days later, George, who sat by the window, slid onto the floor and asked me to join him. I slid down, and after I did so, George rubbed my vagina with his hand. Geoffrey firmly told his brother not to do that to me, and I was glad he did because I didn't know how to say that I didn't like that.

When I got off the bus, I asked my mother if the twins were allowed to kiss me, and she said, "No, no kissing boys."

I explained to my mother that I always kissed Daddy and my uncles and cousins who were boys, so my mother informed me it was okay because I was related to them; it was different to the twins because we're not related. I was so happy that my mother said I wasn't allowed to kiss the twins, and I told them in the morning that kisses weren't allowed.

George asked, "Ah, not even on the cheek?"

I told him that my mother said not even cheek kisses. I didn't want them to kiss me anymore since he touched me in my private area, assuming I would be okay with it. I also didn't want another chance for that to happen again, so telling him that kisses weren't allowed would stop him from doing anything else. I told them I still wanted to be their girlfriend, just not allowed to kiss until I was old enough.

As I expected, Lydia was not a friend to us but a liar and a thief. And not just any thief, a thief that would even steal from their mother. On the bus ride to school one morning, Lydia showed me and Adessa that she borrowed her mother's necklace for school, and I asked, "Your mother let you wear that to school?"

She smiled and said she didn't ask permission since she was only wearing it for the day and would put it back once Lydia was home so her mother wouldn't know she took it in the first place. Later, on the bus ride home, Lydia was panicking. She told Adessa and me that she put the necklace in her backpack and double-checked once we got on the bus to find out she may have lost it. Lydia asked us to think of an excuse for when her mother asked where the necklace was. Adessa told her to say she didn't know, and Lydia said she already asked her mother if she could wear it to school, but her mother said no because someone might steal it since it was expensive gold. I told her to tell her mother the truth. I informed her that my mother taught me to tell her the truth because she wouldn't be as mad as she would have if she found out I told a lie to her.

When we got off the bus, Lydia asked if Adessa and I could go inside her house for a minute so she could show us something. Wishing my mother had said no, we went inside. She showed us her jewelry collection, and then I said I had to go since my mother was waiting outside for me, so Adessa and I left.

A few hours later, after my sister came home from school but before my father came home from work, there was a knock at the door. My mother answered and then yelled for me to get over there. When I got to the door, I saw Lydia and her mother. Her mother stared at me while Lydia wouldn't look at me.

My mother said, "I know you wouldn't have taken jewelry from their house, but did you see Adessa take Lydia's mom's necklace?"

I was furious and said, "What? No, neither one of us took her mother's necklace. She took her mother's necklace to school and lost it."

I looked at Lydia, who still wouldn't look at me, and asked why she lied. While her mother originally came to my mother's house expecting to get her necklace back and an apology, she was now demanding her daughter to apologize to my mother and me. My mother accepted her apology, and they left.

When I told my mother it was jewelry that Lydia wanted to show us, she said, "Oh, that little bitch. She did that so her mother would think she was telling the truth. Well, I bet she didn't count on her mother coming to ask for it back. Only, she didn't get it back 'cause my daughter ain't no thief."

My mother told me that when she answered the door, Lydia's mother had an attitude and said, "Your daughter and her friend stole my necklace, and I want it back." So my mother said, "Um, excuse me? My daughter doesn't steal, and how dare you come to my house accusing my daughter of something."

When Lydia's mother apologized, my mother said she didn't know Adessa too well but she would ask me if I saw anything, and that's when she called me over. I loved how no matter how big a person was, my mother was never afraid to defend her children or anyone she loved for that matter. It was hilarious that no one ever challenged her on it, except for my father, but that never stopped her from defending us. But anyone else my mother stood up to, they were the ones to step down. I wondered if it was her bark or her twitching eye that made them back off. It was always both for me when I'd be the one she was yelling at.

After the shit Lydia had pulled, my mother told me she didn't want me going to her house anymore. I told my mother that was not a problem. As I told my mother how I felt about Lydia, she admitted that she sensed something was off about the girl but wanted to let me choose my friends. Wanting to get off the discussion of Lydia and the headache she caused, my mother asked how my three boyfriends were, and I told her they were fine. I was afraid to tell my mother what George did to me, especially since he didn't do it again. As for Kurt, I let my mother know we barely spoke to each other, so I wasn't sure that we were still boyfriend and girlfriend although neither one of us broke up with the other.

CHAPTER 37

Don't Get Stabbed by Grandpa

In the spring of 1990, my grandfather managed to get himself kicked out of his son Heinrich's house. As my father was excited to have his father home, my mother, sister, and I dreaded it and prayed he would stop his stubborn shit and return to Heinrich's house where he belonged.

The first day he got to our house, he was already starting his shit, acting like he was the boss of the house. It drove me crazy that my father treated my grandfather like a king. He always seemed to think his father was on his deathbed and needed to be taken care of. It made me sick to my stomach when my father expected me to treat my grandfather the same way. It was detrimental to my father that I showed my grandfather who his true and only grandchild was. Now I had to act like I cared that my grandfather loved little Heinrich more than me.

I hated when he made me go to the basement with him while my father was at work. My mother told him she didn't want me down there without my father, but my grandfather claimed he was elderly and needed help up and down the stairs. Thinking she didn't wish the elder to fall and break bones, my mommy decided to let me help him.

My grandfather did the same things to me as the last time he lived with us, putting tape over my mouth and scratching me a little with his pocket knife. I didn't care as long as he didn't touch me like he did when I was a baby. I liked the feeling of tape over my mouth because I had fun attempting to speak with it; my mouth vibrated and tickled. The scratching of the knife Grandpa used on me felt so good that I wished he would push the blade against my skin harder, but the lectures made me hope he would let me go back upstairs. I didn't care about the Germans and how they thought they were the only ones worthy enough to be alive. It wasn't long before he caused my parents to get into arguments so he could laugh on the couch as my father would make my mother have sex.

I loved the days when my grandfather would leave for hours. That was when Adessa could come over, and I wouldn't worry about my grandfather tattling on me to my father. My father didn't want Adessa coming over anymore since his father said I shouldn't be allowed to play with that little slut; they were concerned that hanging out with her would keep me from changing my mind and joining them and their army.

One day, my mother let me play in my room with Adessa, and once Adessa saw how big my sister's boobs had gotten, she ran over and squeezed them as she made honking sounds. My sister smacked her hands away and ran to the kitchen to tell my mother. At that point, I agreed it was time to tell our mommy. My mother told Adessa she had to go home and that she was calling her mother.

When Adessa left, my mother picked up the phone. Adessa's mother was shocked at her behavior and promised my mother it wouldn't happen again, stating she needed to get to the bottom of the situation. It wasn't long until Adessa's mother found out where her daughter learned it and shared the information with my mother, apologizing again for her daughter's behavior. She claimed to my mother that while Adessa was visiting her father on weekends, he was molesting her. She thanked my mother for bringing it to her attention. Otherwise, she may not have found out it was happening.

Also, it wasn't long until I noticed Adessa and her family had moved away, leaving nothing but a box of stuff on the left side of the house. I saw Adessa's stuffed toy pony and asked my father if I could have it. He yelled at me for wanting a slave's garbage and went on and on about that little slut and how he was glad she was gone. I didn't feel that way; I missed my friend and wondered why she didn't tell me they were moving. I had hoped she would call me with her new number, but she didn't. I figured at least my friend won't be molested by her father anymore.

My father and grandfather were mad at my sister and me for an unknown reason, so my father wouldn't take our bikes out of the basement before he left for work. One day, my grandfather decided his granddaughters shouldn't get prevented from getting good exercise, and he convinced my father to let us ride them. Later, as we were riding our bikes around the house, I saw my grandfather walk to the right side of the house, closest to the brown one next to us, which he also considered a welfare house and that only trashy people lived there.

My sister and I passed him, and as we came around again, I saw my grandfather pulling his knife out of his pocket and opening the blade; the next round, as my sister passed him, he acted as if he would stab her in her side until she was out of his reach. He then smiled at me as I followed behind my sister and did the same thing to me.

I laughed, figuring this was probably one of his stupid games, and I wouldn't have minded getting stabbed since I needed to feel pain. As we passed him a few times without my sister noticing what our grandfather was doing, she caught him and screamed, being he was pretty close to her with a sharp knife. He laughed and did the same to me, so I laughed and kept following my sister around the house again, except this time she stopped and hopped off her bike by the back door then ran toward me and made my bike stop. She helped me off my bike, grabbed my hand, and we ran inside the house.

We ran to my mother, and my sister frantically told her what happened. I had never seen my mother's eyes get as wide as I did that day. She screamed for my grandfather to get inside so they could talk about him trying to stab her daughters. My grandfather didn't come inside, so my mother went to the back door and swung it open while yelling, "Who the fuck do you think you are trying to stab my girls?" She pointed at him as he stood by the bottom of the stairs, saying,

"Don't you ever fucking pull that shit again, and just wait until your son finds out."

My grandfather acted as if he did nothing wrong, claiming he was only playing around and would not have stabbed us. My mother didn't accept his excuse and said, "Not that I should have to tell you this, Will, but you do not play with sharp objects and point them at children, especially while riding their bikes."

She explained that while Ada was a great rider, I had only learned the summer before, and I hadn't ridden it since summer had ended. She asked what he would have done if one of us had gotten hurt. Tired of hearing her bitch and complain, my grandfather told my mother to go fuck herself and for her to wait until his son was home. He was sure my father would be on his side, and he went to the front yard to sit in his Lincoln Town Car until his son returned home from work. It was like déjà vu when my father came storming into the house, demanding answers as to why his father got kicked out and was living in his car in the front for all the neighbors to see.

My mother informed my father that she didn't kick him out and that he went of his own free will. Once she told my father what his father did to their girls and how their children could have gotten hurt or worse, he changed his tone and stormed outside to speak with his dear old dad. When my father came back inside the house, he asked my mother if she minded if his father stayed until he found another place to go or when he could go to Heinrich's. Appreciating being asked for once, my mother agreed but said he was not allowed in the house while my father was at work and would have to visit other family or something.

My father went back outside to see why his father hadn't come inside and to let him know he was allowed to stay a little longer. My grandfather, being the stubborn man he was, would not go back in unless my mother came out and apologized for yelling at him like he was a child. My father knew that would not happen, so he told me to come out with him and convince Grandpa that he couldn't stay outside and should come inside. I followed my father and asked my grandfather if I could sit in his car with him. He agreed and let me in. I acted as if I was so concerned for my grandfather's health and begged him to come back inside. The truth was, I wished he would die already so he would be out of my way of trying to save my father from following the wrong path. I couldn't have cared less if he stayed in his car or died there.

One day while my father was in the basement showing me the tools his father let him hold onto, I could see the hurt in his eyes. He knew what his father had done was wrong, but he felt guilty for asking him to leave, especially knowing he'd go crawling back to my uncle Heinrich's house. Thinking of what I could do to change my father's mind about missing his father, I grabbed an open roll of duct tape and put some over my mouth while trying to talk. As I intended to get him to laugh and be happy again, something else happened. My father realized I could only have learned that from one person, my dear old grandpa.

Now, instead of him wishing his father would come back, he was bitching about that being done to me as well as now I was wasting his duct tape. Being told not to put it over my mouth only made me want to do it some more. When my father cut the piece off, he put it down on the table while he put the roll of duct tape out of my reach and moved all his other rolls of tape up as well. I grabbed the piece of tape I already used, figuring I wouldn't be wasting something that was already a waste, and I put it back over my mouth.

When my father turned to me and saw I was at it again, he ripped it off and threw it in the garbage while yelling, "Cut that shit out. You like being a slave, don't you? You disgust me. Get the fuck outta here. Go upstairs by your slut mother."

I gladly obeyed, and as I walked through the kitchen, I stopped at the junk drawer to grab the scotch tape and brought it to my room. My sister eventually came in and saw what I was doing. I looked at her and began trying to talk to her. She started laughing and suggested we go to show our mother. Our mother did find it funny and said how I do strange things sometimes that she couldn't help but laugh at. She asked that I take it easy with the tape since she wasn't sure when King David would be willing to waste his money on another roll.

Then my mother said, "Whatever you do, don't ever let your father see you playing with the tape."

I told my mother, "I already did, and he yelled at me. That's why I'm back in the house. He made me come in."

She rolled her eyes at how cheap and strict my father was and said, "It's okay, you stay by Mommy then. Stay away from that crank until he gets the bug out of his ass."

My sister added, "He always has a bug up his butt."

We all laughed together at the constant crank of a man's expense.

CHAPTER 38

Ms. Mato Hates Goodbyes, and So Do I

As I wished I never had to leave Ms. Mato and the kindergarten school, the school year was nearing the end, which meant saying goodbye. She had told us throughout the year how great we were and that she loved being our teacher. But now she was saying things that made me want to cry. Ms. Mato told us how much she hated goodbyes, and I thought, *So do I.* She thanked us for making this a great year and said how much she would miss us.

I thought about how I felt before school started. Without knowing what it would be like, I assumed I would hate the school and everyone who would be inside. I remembered how happy I was when I saw the teacher lets white kids play with black baby dolls and when she taught me about the Indians. I could never forget Ms. Mato or the way she showed compassion for many of the things I wasn't allowed to know about at home. I knew I would remember how she introduced herself to the class and that when I felt sad about the name I chose for myself, she helped me feel better about it and keep it.

Having to say goodbye to Ms. Mato when the last day came was so hard and painful, but I counted my blessings for being able to say goodbye. When I had to leave Joseph and Lynette, I got to say goodbye, but I never got to say goodbye to Uncle Hans or Aunt Maple. I didn't get a chance to say goodbye to Bowie. And when Imani's family left and then Adessa's family, I didn't even know they were leaving me until they were already gone. It made me feel like I had a big hole inside me for each person I would never see again, and it would never close.

Knowing that I could say goodbye to Ms. Mato made it much easier to get through the emotional time. It wasn't until that night before I went to sleep that I finally let the tears flow. And this time, when Ada asked why I was crying, I was relieved to know I was allowed to tell her why so she wouldn't say I was crying for no reason. She understood that I was crying for a good reason. My sister didn't like seeing me upset and wanted me to feel better about having to leave my teacher. She told me I would go to her school once it was open, and we would be on the bus together. I asked if our classes would be close to each other's, and she explained my grade would be in a different area of the school than hers. As she tried to explain the layout, I didn't understand her, but I loved it when my sister helped me learn things; she was intelligent and a great teacher. I let her explain all she felt she needed to.

I told her I was worried about going to the elementary school because of what happened to her in that school when she was on the playground one day. The kids had gone out for recess, and my sister accidentally bumped into a black boy from another class. He pulled a knife out of his pocket and pointed it toward her, so she ran like hell to get away from him and didn't go near him again. My sister told me I didn't have to worry about that happening to me and that if it did, I could let her know and she would protect me. I wanted to believe her, but she didn't protect me from our cousins when they harmed me. Although she did save me from Grandpa trying to stab us. I didn't want to make my sister feel bad, so I agreed to go to her if I needed her protection. Our heart-to-heart meant the world to me regardless, and I thanked my sister for cheering me up.

She smiled and said, "See ya in the morning, Napoleon."

I smiled back and replied, "Good night, Lafayette."

*****

Every year, on the day school ended, my mother would take us to our grandma's house where Anja, OJ, and my sister would run around singing, "No more pencils, no more books, no more teacher's dirty looks, kick the tables, kick the chairs, kick the teacher down the stairs. Hope the stairs are made of glass, hope the teacher breaks her ass."

In the past, I liked the song, and I loved running around with my cousins. It was fun, and for the moment, they weren't making me do sex stuff or teasing me. But this year, I went by my mother and cried because I missed Ms. Mato. Learning her name, OJ sang the song, but instead of saying teacher, he'd say Ms. Mato.

When my mother had enough of his shit, picking on me and hurting my feelings, she told my grandmother she had to leave before she would end up smacking OJ right across his damn face. That day, I was so happy that OJ didn't get to make me do sex stuff, but the next time we went, I wasn't allowed to play with Anja and my sister since my aunt told me I had to be "seen" but not heard. I wondered if she knew how stupid she sounded. How could anyone be seen on another level of the house and behind not one but two closed doors? It was hard holding back what I wanted to say to her since I could remember, but knowing I would probably have to eat a whole bar of soap, I said it in my head, *You stupid, fat, fucking bitch, we aren't seen or heard. Get off your lazy ass and come see what happens when you say that.*

I wished the school would hurry up and open back up; I did not want to spend my summer doing sexual things with my cousin every time I visited my grandmother's house. But I also was not looking forward to attending a school where kids try to stab kids. Plus, my father informed me that while I didn't have many eyes on me in kindergarten, that would change at my next school and every school after that. There wasn't a safe place I could go to where no one would hurt me, tease me, or make me do sex stuff. I was tired of not being loved enough. I wished the world would change. It has to change. I needed to do what God told my heart to tell my brain. I had to find good people and speak in a code to spread the word about my family without getting caught, or people I loved would die. Maybe even myself. I wondered if my death would be such a bad thing after all.

EPILOGUE

Many people wondered how my father could be so cruel, yet I still loved him unconditionally, just as much as my mother. My cousins would ask me or I would hear the grown-ups talk about it when they thought I couldn't hear. Some would say that I loved my father more than my mother because I would not dare speak to my father the way I did to my mother. When I would hear Aunt Greta say things like that, I wondered if she was trying to make my mother hate me, and that made me wonder why she would do that. Why would she agree that my father was cruel and then turn around and tell him something that would make him beat me later when he could?

Life was so exhausting, but I held the good memories closest to my heart to survive the deadly trauma I faced daily since before I could remember. While my father was horrible, sometimes he was a great father. Sometimes, he was such a great father that even my sister would laugh and have a good time with us. Going to the park, he would grill up some food, or we'd bring things to make sandwiches. He would take us to the playground or the meadow where we would play ball in an open space. Like at home, in our backyard, we played a game where he would kick the ball so high in the sky. My sister and I would have to try and catch it, and whoever caught the ball would earn one dollar.

Then he'd ask, "You want to double it?" Sometimes the question would be "Double or nothing?" which meant you had to try for double or forfeit and get nothing.

My father once was so kind that he took us to see the horses, and I wanted to ride the pony, but as soon as I got on, I was scared. My sister tried to convince me it was fun, but I felt dizzy and cried to get down. The lady that walked on the side of the pony took me down and told me I was welcome to come back and try any time. My father also loved taking us for family walks around the neighborhood or to the playgrounds when schools were closed. There are many good memories with my father, but unfortunately, the bad outweighed the good since even the good times sometimes changed into bad ones.

Playing with us, my father would still do things to turn my sister and me against each other. Or he'd suddenly become cranky and end the game, calling us names and saying we were too young to play. I was too stupid, or my sister was too fat. He didn't know how to have a good time and end it that way. But even at such a young age, I knew that was what my grandfather and my great-grandfather did to him, and old habits are hard to break. It became normal for my father when he was very young.

The answer to the question if I loved my father more than my mother is no, absolutely not. I carried the burden of knowing their traumatic childhoods and gave them all the love I could. And while my mother's childhood was traumatic, my father's was more severe. He needed my attention more than my mother did. I needed to give him double the love and affection my father didn't get from birth. I needed him to change his ways and apologize to God so my father could go to heaven when he died. I didn't have to guide my mother toward the right path in life since she was already heading in that direction.

ABOUT THE AUTHOR

I am a human, yet I have never felt I am. I had to be German in a united country, the United States of America, land of the free, when I have never been free, and home of the brave, where most of everyone I knew and loved was a bunch of cowards following the path of the devil. Weighing barely 7 lbs. and having grown men and women whom I had no choice but to surrender, molding me into "royalty" was painful. Being told to love and respect the ones who do nothing but cause me harm and to disrespect the people who love, nurture, and protect me was undeniably confusing.

I am German, Irish, Indian, and Dutch, from what I remember hearing, but I was to be German. I was to obey my father and our fathers before him, even the deceased ones. I was born what my paternal family thinks is a "chosen one" to their God, who is in fact the devil. I could hear so many names of supposed great leaders, some of whom I was told were my ancestors that I must avenge. Two figures I can never forget, no matter how much I was trafficked and drugged, were William Floyd and Adolf Hitler.

I developed hyperthymesia, a gift and a curse in itself. I can remember much of my life and the traumatic events I endured, as well as my loved ones who also suffered abuse, and I can remember as far back as not even age two. As young as I was, I knew all this was wrong. Why should I hate someone because of the color hair or eyes they were born with, or why should I abuse someone just because their skin is not white like mine? And why would I even want to respect those who do not respect me or the people I love? So I made a vow before even turning two that I must save my father, the man to whom I was born.

He, like all the others so confused and misguided, truly believes that there is no such thing as heaven or hell. The family I was born into had taught me that reincarnation does not exist and that only the truest Germans will God resurrect at the end of days, yet I knew this was not true at all. This and more are the reasons I never, even for a second, felt human. I consider myself a hybrid; I am different from most. I am unique and colorful. I know what my purpose in life is. I need to save as many survivors as possible. Most girls dream of becoming a teacher or a ballerina, but I hoped to be a hero who saves the world. I knew it would not be easy, but I did not care. The world needs to change, and I need to stop my father from going to the very dark world he refuses to admit exists.

I know my mother went to heaven and also that my father will be burning in Satan's flames if he does not once and for all listen to his daughter. A therapist I used to see once asked me if I was in a room with ten other people, who is most important. I answered all of us. Of course, she said I was wrong; my answer should have been me. I believe she was wrong; I am no more or less important than anyone. Every person is born with a purpose and a gift; we deserve to be loved and respected.

As a child, I also wanted to learn how to write a novel to expose the evil hidden right under everyone's noses. Hyperthymesia is not my only gift. Long ago, I'd be called a witch and burned to death. I have seen what will become of us if people do not change for the good; I can vouch for a psychic, whom I have never met, who publicly predicted the future. Their visions were not false; I have seen them myself. While people desperately need to gain followers for popularity on social media, I would like to have followers for a better world.

As I grew and lost faith in God, he stuck by my side and guided me while so many people were misguiding me. I've always wondered if natural disasters are God's warning to the evil that roams the earth, but what I do know is that if the world does end, all the good people will go to heaven. He loves you even if you are gay. He loves you if you are not as pretty as your neighbor. God loves you even if you are a man and decide you want to be a woman. God does not judge if you want to dress like a pony and frolic in the meadow. He does not mind if you want to be boorishly normal. As much as I would love to attend a church, I cannot because I cannot hear a preacher say that same-sex partnership is an unforgivable sin. I was angry when I heard a pastor say that if you use drugs or alcohol, you will not go to heaven. None of that is true; God loves all his children. He even loves the ones so deep into the darkness that there is no chance of turning to good, but those people are the ones he has no choice but to deny entry to a real paradise island. Instead, they have to go to eternal life in hell with Lucifer.

Printed in the USA
CPSIA information can be obtained
at www.ICGtesting.com
LVHW051937121124
796384LV00002B/190